What Will You Create?

Drawing with the 3Doodler®

CONTENTS

CONTENTS

Maxwell Bogue

Daniel Cowen

Pete Dilworth

Portraits: Erin Song

The story of the 3Doodler began in a cramped cubicle in the Artisan's Asylum Maker Space in Somerville, MA. One fine spring day in 2012 our 3D printer had almost finished a 14 hour print when disaster struck. It had missed a line in the print and we were going to have to start again.

That's when inspiration struck: What if we could just take off the print head and fill in the gap by hand?

A day later we were craned over a clumsy looking device fondly called *the teacup*, extruding plastic through a series of gears, a heater and the print head of our now extinct 3D printer. The words *3Doodler* were etched onto its side in green and red felt tip pen. The first 3Doodler – and a whole new creative medium – was born.

In less than a year – February 2013 – we launched our first Kickstarter campaign, sharing our dream with the world, asking tens of thousands of people who we had never met to help make that dream a reality. Over 25,000 backers pre-ordered a 3Doodler, with tens of thousands more following in their footsteps in the months after. At the time of going to print we have shipped over 300,000 3Doodlers, to every corner of the globe.

In the past two and half years we haven't just created the 3Doodler – we have also built an incredible team of over twenty people, each one of them working hard every day to make the 3Doodler even better and to inspire our creative community to reach even greater heights. And yet, despite our constant efforts to raise the bar, more often than not, it's the things that you – our community – do, that inspire us the most.

From the very first prototype of the 3Doodler (with all it's stop-start) to the new silky-smooth 3Doodler 2.0, our talented and engaged community of artists, educators, and tech lovers have inspired us beyond belief, constantly pushing the boundaries of what we thought was possible. If there's a way to use the 3Doodler that we haven't thought of yet, we know you'll find it!

This book, first and foremost, is for all of you: It is a guide for anyone picking up the 3Doodler for the very first time asking, 'what shall I create?' or 'how can I make that!?'. It is also a platform for any experienced Doodler looking for inspiration and challenges to take their skills to the next level.

The introductory Bootcamp with three drills and 26 step-by-step projects have been carefully crafted to get you Doodling as soon as possible, from the simple to the complex. The stunning images of 3Doodled creations, coupled with our vibrant Community Site are there to awe, inspire – and we hope, eventually be surpassed by –your own amazing creativity.

We would like to say thank you to everyone who has helped bring this book to fruition: To all of the talented artists we have worked with over the years and who have contributed to this book (you can find their profiles on page 154) – thank you for inspiring us and for letting us shine a light on your work.

To Vickie and Josh, for the many hours spent getting this book into shape (what were we thinking, getting into publishing?), Abigail Rubenstein for her proofreading and advice, and to the whole 3Doodler team, we are so grateful for all of your hard work, devotion and the joy you bring to this crazy rollercoaster ride! To the 3Doodler community, we hope to inspire and delight you as much as you inspire and delight us. And finally to our friends, family and everyone else who has touched our worlds and supported us on this journey, we could not have done this without each and every one of you.

Now it's over to you, to enjoy, create and share what you make with your 3Doodler!

Max, Dan & Pete

INTRODUCTION

Imagine a pen that you can literally lift off the page to create real three dimensional objects; a pen that puts the power of 3D creation in the palm of your hand. If you are holding a 3Doodler right now, then you don't have to imagine any more.

What exactly is the 3Doodler? Compact and easy to use, the 3Doodler is a pen that extrudes heated plastic that cools almost instantly into a solid, stable structure. Without the need for a computer or software, the possibilities are limited only by your imagination. Simply plug your 3Doodler into a power socket and start drawing anything, within minutes.

To create the 3Doodler, we took elements from the world of 3D printing and streamlined them so that you could hold them in your hand – in fact, so that you could start creating quickly and easily. In the words of Ecco Pierce, one of the first artists we worked with, "the barrier between you and your idea is very thin." If you can imagine it, you can create it.

Most people will instantly be able to use the 3Doodler to trace objects on paper and after only a few hours of practice, be able to make far more intricate objects. Just load in some plastic, push the button and begin.

Since we first showed the world that drawing in 3D was possible, our community has been using 3Doodlers to create amazing things, going far beyond even our wildest expectations.

The 3Doodler has applications for designers, artists, crafters, architects, engineers, educators and 3D print enthusiasts – both commercial and recreational. It can be used for home or industrial repairs, to make artistic objects, to teach geometry and spatial relations to students – it's even been used to make raised line graphs and hand written Braille by people in the blind and low vision community.

This book was written with the aim of opening up that world of creativity to everyone. Starting with a technique tutorial and a Bootcamp, this book will take you through the basic techniques that will help you Doodle for years to come. Armed with your 3Doodler and ready to go, try the step-by-step projects, from the simple to the complex, ranging from the decorative to the playful – and even the wearable. We've also included some photos of some of our favorite Doodles from around the 3Doodler world. We hope these inspire you as much as they did us.

The world of 3Doodler doesn't end here: We have a vibrant online community and we're constantly working on new technology, materials and accessories to take your 3Doodling to the next level. There are already four types of filaments available for the 3Doodler: ABS, PLA, WOOD (which is made of 20 percent wood fiber) and FLEXY (which true to its name, is very flexible like rubber). There is also a nozzle set with six different nozzles, each of which produces different types of lines.

We hope that this book helps and inspires you to push the boundaries of 3D creation and art making – and that you have as much fun using it as we had creating it.

#WhatWillYouCreate?™

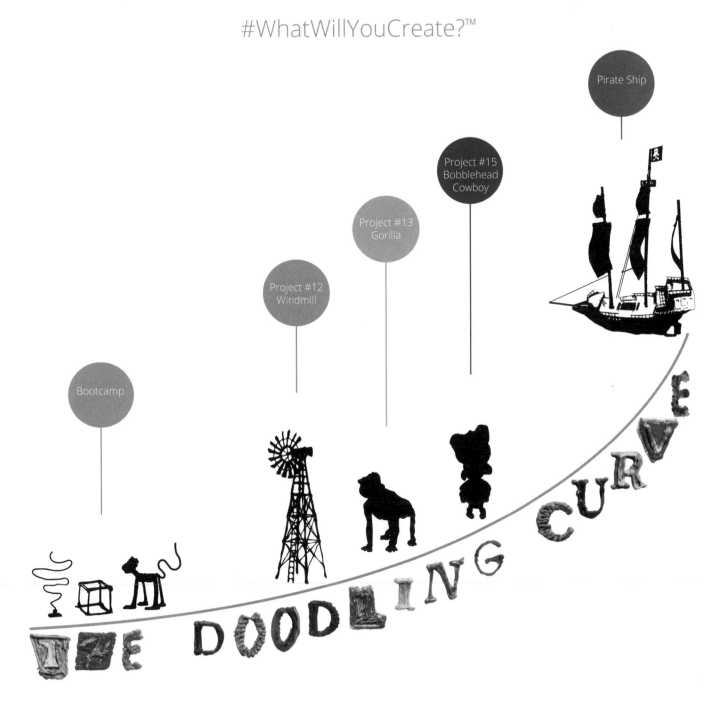

| Getting to know the 3Doodler | Working up your skills | Getting creative | Doodle Master |

Doodle skill

Esra Oguz

Getting Started

In this book you will find a 3Doodler Bootcamp with basic techniques that will get you ready for the 26 exciting step-by-step projects that follow, each shared by our network of expert Doodlers.

Some projects are easier and some more challenging; some take less time and some take more – but time doesn't necessarily relate to how difficult the project is. We've made this book easy to learn with, so the simpler projects are found at the front and the more complex towards the end. Some include stencils for you to follow. For those who love holidays, there's also a dedicated chapter at the back of the book, which includes both easy and challenging holiday projects.

Glossary

Before you start, here's a glossary of terms that you might want to refer back to, as needed. It will help you to understand some of the special Doodling terms used throughout the book.

Plastic filaments for the 3Doodler

ABS – ABS plastic is one of the strongest plastics available for the 3Doodler. It cools faster and hardens more quickly. It is good for better control and sturdier vertical lines. This makes it the preferred plastic for many beginners.

PLA – A corn-based bio-plastic, it can be shaped and bent for about five seconds after it cools, and looks shinier once it dries. PLA is more brittle than ABS, but it holds much better to other materials, like paper, glass, or metal. It also comes in stunning transparent colors.

FLEXY – A rubberized, elastic plastic that stays flexible long after it cools. FLEXY can be used to make bendable figures, clothing, ribbons, straps and even a wallet that you can use, like the one in Project #2 on page 24.

WOOD – Made from approximately 20 percent wood fiber mixed with PLA, WOOD looks like real wood, smells like real wood and can be used to make items that need a wooden finish. WOOD can also be used to touch up real wooden items or it can be sanded down or stained.

NOTE: There is no clear rule about which plastic is better – they each have unique features that make them better suited to certain tasks. Experiment and see which you prefer!

Other terms

Anchor – When you start to extrude plastic, you will need to anchor the plastic to your Doodling surface. To do so, gently but firmly push down with the nozzle so that the plastic sticks to the surface. You can then lift up and Doodle in the air.

Armature – Sometimes you need to Doodle a frame, known as an armature, to build your more complex 3D structures upon. You can do this free hand or base it on a stencil.

Bead or Beading – To ensure a firm anchor, you can create a 'bead' of plastic by letting it flow for a moment on the spot, forming a bead on the surface. This makes for a strong base to Doodle from.

Coil or Coiling – Used to create a sturdy structure, coiling is when you Doodle circles on top of each other to create a taller coiled structure. You can coil freely, or alternatively Doodle some straight lines or shapes and then coil around them in tight or wide circles, stacking them one above the other, like a coil.

NOTE: To learn more about the relationship between the flow of plastic – or extrusion speed – and your hand and wrist movement, see Extrusion speed and Flow, below.

Doodling surface – A suitable surface on which you can Doodle. This might be paper, cardboard, plastic that won't melt under the heat of the 3Doodler nozzle, or an object that isn't precious (in case it gets damaged). Note that PLA sticks firmly to normal paper. To prevent this, you can cover your paper with sellotape or masking tape, from which the PLA will peel away more easily. Do not cover your paper with a thin plastic like cling wrap, which will melt easily.

WARNING: Never Doodle against exposed skin.

Extrusion speed – The speed of the flow of plastic coming from the 3Doodler. See Flow, below.

NOTE: There is an important relationship between the extrusion speed or flow and your hand and wrist movement. Practice makes perfect – you will soon develop a natural feel for it.

Fill or Filling – Doodles often start with an outline, which needs filling in. Simply fill the empty space inside the lines, for instance, with a side-to-side (zig-zag) line – or whatever style you prefer.

Flow – The flow of plastic coming from the 3Doodler. Also see Extrusion speed, above.

Layer or Layering – Sometimes a single layer of plastic isn't enough, so Doodling over it again makes it thicker, higher, stronger, more stable or heavier. You can layer to infinity and beyond.

Stencil – Using a stencil not only makes some projects easier to follow, but as you create your own Doodles, stencils will help you to plan ahead and ensure all the parts fit together well. You can download stencils from the website, or, create your own using a pencil and paper or objects lying around your home including photos. Projects that include stencils are marked with an S on the page tab.

Find stencils at
the3Doodler.com/create/

String or Stringing – Moving the pen across an open space from one point on a Doodle to another, or between your Doodle and another item. Think of how a spider weaves a web.

Weld or Welding – You will often need to weld Doodled pieces together. The 3Doodler's nozzle is hot and will melt plastic, helping you to weld things together. You can also use extruded plastic from the 3Doodler to weld other plastics/objects together (including your broken remote control)!

Wind or Winding – To form rounded shapes like spheres and balls, it is sometimes easier to wind plastic around an object like a ball, water bottle or a balled up piece of (tissue) paper that is the right size for your project. Doodle around the object, creating overlapping lines that build up to form a spherical shape. As the sphere takes shape, you can remove the tissue and use the already Doodled lines as your guide.

There are no rights and wrongs in the world of Doodling and you may invent a few techniques of your own – but the glossary and techniques explained above will give you a great skillset to begin with.

So, are you ready for Bootcamp?

Welcome to Bootcamp!

It's time to put you through your paces and teach you the basics that will pave the way towards making you a Doodle master. You will be presented with three fun and easy drills. They will feel simple, but they will teach you the fundamentals you will need to make much more complex and intricate pieces later on.

If you feel like it, practice each a few times and play around with the pen until it starts to feel natural in your hand. Ready? Let's get started!

Bootcamp Drill #1: Cube

In this drill, we're going to make a cube.

Basic shapes are the fundamental building blocks of even the most complex structures, so let's start with something easy. Once you're comfortable with the simpler shapes, you can use this technique to make any geometric design – no matter how large or intricate.

1. Pressing firmly, draw a one inch (2.5 cm) square on your Doodling surface. This will form the foundation and underside of your cube. Reinforce the shape by tracing over it again.

2. From each corner, Doodle a one inch (2.5 cm) vertical line, as illustrated. To Doodle each vertical line, pull up while extruding and then release the extrusion button when you reach the desired height. Hold the 3Doodler in place for 2-3 seconds, allowing the plastic to harden and then pull away.

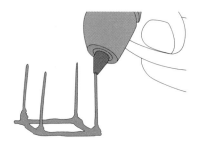

3. Connect the top of the vertical lines by Doodling from point to point, creating a square that sits above the underside of the cube. This is the top of the cube.

4. Once you have connected all four top corners, reinforce the whole cube by Doodling another layer of plastic over it. Now your cube is sturdy and ready to stand on its own.

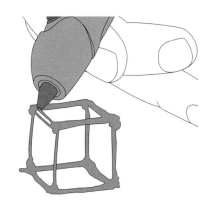

Not done with this bootcamp drill? Practice the technique in different sizes and colors – or experiment to see what other shapes you can make!

Bootcamp Drill #2: Squiggly Tower

This drill will teach you how to make structures that stand on their own, so you can explore the fundamentals of free hand drawing and creating Doodles in mid-air.

1. Pressing firmly to anchor the plastic to your Doodling surface, draw the outline of a one inch (2.5 cm) square and shade it in fully, by moving the pen back and forth diagonally.

2. After shading in the base square, repeat, adding a second layer of plastic. This creates a strong foundation for your Doodle and allows you to make tall creations that will not easily tip over.

3. In the center of your square, begin to build up the base of the tower by tightly coiling the plastic as it extrudes.

4. Build up your coil until it is about one inch (2.5 cm) high and then move your hand upwards with a smooth sweeping motion from side to side. By doing this, you can begin to explore the relationship between extrusion speed and the movement of your hands and wrists.

You have the ability to create flowing 3D shapes and draw in mid-air! Cut the flow when you have finished Doodling and voilà – you have created a squiggly tower!

TIP: The coiling technique is an essential method for making stable vertical structures that are strong, straight and able to support larger Doodles.

TIP: Learning the relationship between extrusion speed (flow) and the movement of your hands and wrists is key to becoming great at Doodling! Learn more about the terms, in the Glossary on page 12.

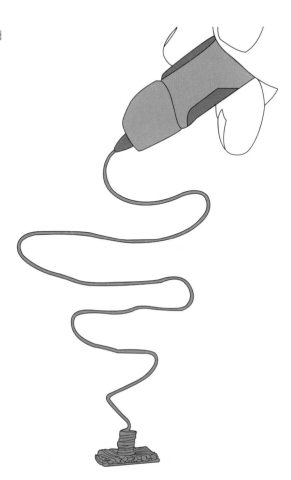

Now that you've made some abstract shapes, it's time to make something real: The Doodle Dog (or 3Poodle).

Bootcamp Drill #3: Doodle Dog

This cute little guy is quick and easy to make – and will get you ready to create almost any creature or character you can dream up!

NOTE: It's a good idea to read all of the instructions a few times before you start, because it's best to try not to cut the flow of plastic unless clearly instructed. This way, your dog will look neater. If you need to, practice certain steps or movements a few times, separately.

1. Doodle the outline of a small oval on your Doodling surface. This will form the dog's back, right paw. Fill it in so that it is firmly attached to the surface and has a nice rounded shape. Next, bring the pen up at a slight angle to create the first leg.

2. Continuing in one fluid motion, loop back down towards the paper so that the plastic forms a tight arch – now the dog has both back legs. Attach the second back paw to the paper and fill it in (see the first half of step 1, if you need help).

3. Reinforce the legs by tracing over them a few times fluidly, finishing with the pen at the top of the arch. From this point, Doodle a tight horizontal coil to form the dog's body. Ideally, his body should be a little shorter in length, than his legs.

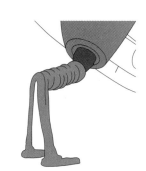

4. The end of the horizontal coil forms the dog's front shoulders. From there, Doodle downwards to make the first front leg, then Doodle the paw, attaching it to the Doodling surface.

5. Next, trace back up along the leg to make an arch and Doodle down to make the second front leg and paw. Reinforce the front legs by tracing over them a few times, ideally in one fluid flow.

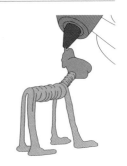

6. To create the dog's neck, Doodle a short, tight coil diagonally upward from the dog's shoulders. At the front end of the coil, Doodle an oval shape to create his head, with two little bumps to form his ears.

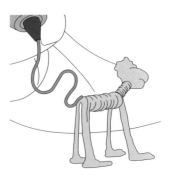

7. Stop the flow of plastic and disconnect, then move the pen to the rear of his body and resume the flow of plastic, pressing gently to attach it. Doodle his tail any shape you want!

Good work!

TIP: You can use the objects around you to help create the shapes you want. For instance, in step 2, you can Doodle over a pen to help form a perfect arch where the Doodle Dog's legs meet.

Louis DeRosa

NOZZLES

Much in the same way that a painter might use different brushes to get the right stroke, the 3Doodler has interchangeable nozzles to give you more flexibility in the style and look of the Doodles you create. Each nozzle gives you a different shape and flow of plastic as it extrudes – which means greater versatility and precision in crafting your Doodles!

The 3Doodler nozzle set contains six different nozzles that vary in size and shape, including a ribbon tip, square tip and triangle tip as well as a 0.5mm, 1mm and 1.5mm tip. A handy tool for quickly changing the nozzles is included, and the handle contains a neat compartment that stores them all. There's also a smoothing tool that clips onto the end of any nozzle, enabling you to smooth over, contour, shape and sculpt your Doodles as they cool.

Ribbon tip: This nozzle extrudes a flat ribbon of plastic, which is useful for shading in flat spaces and for creating ribbon-like shapes. The ribbon nozzle is also ideal for creating the sides of structures like buildings, or thick flowing lines in mid-air.

Square tip: This square-shaped nozzle is great for making geometric shapes and structures and anything with a right-angle. The thick extrusion ensures a stable base for any Doodle. The square tip is ideal for Doodling structural supports and posts.

Triangle tip: This nozzle extrudes a triangular flow of plastic – twist it to create interesting angles and fun visual effects. Triangles are one of the strongest building shapes, so this nozzle is great for making Doodles that need to be stable or structurally sound.

0.5mm tip: This nozzle is for fine detail work. It is 0.2mm smaller than the standard nozzle (included with the 3Doodler) and offers more control when making detailed Doodles like portraits and line drawings or putting the final touches and accents on Doodles.

1mm tip: This nozzle gives you a thicker line of plastic. It is 0.3mm bigger than the standard nozzle (included with the 3Doodler), so it's good for those bigger Doodles and bolder lines. The plastic also flows out of the pen more quickly.

1.5mm tip: The largest nozzle available (over double the size of the standard nozzle), the 1.5mm nozzle is great for shading in large spaces (especially more quickly) or making really big Doodles with strong or highly visible lines. Note that the plastic takes longer to cool because the flow is thick.

With these options, you can make specific choices when creating your Doodle – and of course a Doodle can use more than one nozzle. If you play around with them, you will soon start spontaneously and naturally choosing the right nozzle for your Doodle. Imagine what you can create with so much freedom in line, texture and styles!

Details show off creative prowess:
The Flower Fox was Doodled with all six nozzles.

Whether you are new to the 3Doodler or an experienced Doodle master, one of the most valuable tools for getting your Doodles right, is a stencil.

There are lots more on our website. And once you get the hang of it, you can start to design your own stencils!

Project #1: Butterfly

You will need the stencil provided here to make the butterfly. We suggest you photocopy it, or download it from the website and then cover it in masking tape to form your Doodling surface. PLA and other plastics will stick easily to paper.

Find stencils at
the3Doodler.com/create/

1. First, trace the wing pattern for each wing, following the stencil. Here, we've used black.

2. Then, fill the insides of the wing pattern with any color you want. Here, we've used purple, yellow and blue.

3. When you've finished, carefully remove both wings from your Doodling surface.

4. Next, trace the outline of the body. Fill it in and then layer it up to make a nice, rounded shape, as illustrated.

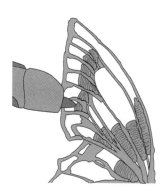

5. Starting at the top of the head, free hand the antennae – or leave them out if you don't want them.

6. Now, attach the wings. To do so, gently hold one wing against the body at an angle (unless you want a flat butterfly) and use the plastic to weld it to the body. That is, Doodle the wing to the body.

   This can be tricky at first, but the hot pen nozzle will melt the plastic together. Repeat to attach the second wing, but be careful not to break the first wing.

Well done! Your butterfly is now ready to emerge from its cocoon and take flight!

TIP: If you want to make your butterfly even prettier, use a clear plastic (we suggest Clearly Clear PLA) to fill in the empty gaps in the wing. You can even Doodle a different color decoration onto the butterfly's body. Be sure to work on the wings before attaching them to the body, to prevent any possible damage.

Nikka Francisco

PROJECT #2: WALLET

For your second project, you are going to make something you can use every day – a wallet, made from FLEXY plastic. This will show that Doodling is a quirky and useful skill!

Project #2: Wallet

You will need the stencil provided here to make the wallet. We suggest you photocopy it, or download it from the website and then cover it in masking tape to form your Doodling surface. PLA and other plastics will stick easily to paper.

Find stencils at
the3Doodler.com/create/

1. Using any color FLEXY you want – black will look more like real leather at a glance – trace the three big rectangles in the stencil and then fill them in. Note that if you Doodle over a surface like glass, you will have a smoother texture on the outside of your wallet.

2. Weld the three rectangles together by Doodling them with plastic. Be sure that one smooth side is on the outside of the wallet and the other two smooth sides are facing inward, towards each other. This will help the bank notes slip in and out easily.

3. Make four small rectangles as shown in the stencil and fill them in. These form the two pockets that will hold your cards.

4. Place as many cards as you want to keep in each pocket, inbetween two of the rectangles with the smooth sides facing inward toward each other, so the cards slip in and out easily. Weld the two rectangles together along the sides.

   You can make the pockets as thick as you want, for as many cards as you want. When you have finished welding the sides together, remove your cards. If you want to add more pockets, you can, by following steps 3 and 4.

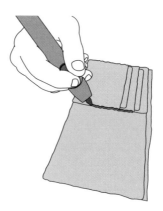

5. Place a piece of paper inside the notes section of the wallet to prevent the heat of the nozzle welding it together as you attach the card pockets to the wallet. Now, weld the card pockets to the wallet by Doodling around the edge of them with a few lines of plastic.

You can use your Doodle as a real wallet! Why not customize it with your initials, or any design you want?

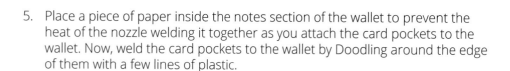

TIP: When you lay down a flat sheet of Doodled plastic like in step 1, or when filling in, your bottom side will have the texture of your Doodling surface because the warm plastic will meld around it. That means you can get a rough texture from certain types of paper and wood, or a smooth surface from glass.

TIP: If your wallet starts to wear out, simply repair it with more FLEXY!

S

Kiwib Wong

x3

x4, or more, for more pockets

PROJECT #3: MIXED MEDIA

Crafting, sculpture, three dimensional art and making great stuff is just what the 3Doodler is built for!

Project #3: Mixed Media

Did you know that the plastic the 3Doodler extrudes will bond to most materials as it's Doodled? You can work with wood, metal, multiple plastics, string, yarn, fabric, glass and even old appliances or working toys!

It means you can be creative with what you make – just look for new materials at a craft store – where you can also look for inspiration. Things around your house, garage and garden can come in handy, too.

Unleash your creativity, whether you're making useable Doodles or just things that look interesting – or, incorporate real world items and make functional items, too. We've seen sculptures, key chains, earrings, decorations and household items, as well as Doodles that incorporate electronics – like remote control helicopters or drones.

Rachel Goldsmith

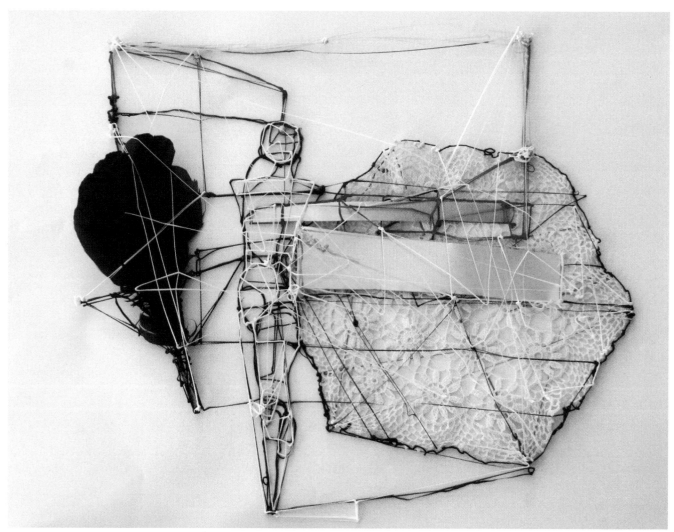

Sara Berti

Matthew Butchard

Esra Oguz

Esra Oguz

SHIGO

One of the best things about the 3Doodler is that after the plastic you've Doodled has hardened, you can use the heat of the nozzle to melt it and weld new parts to objects you've already made. This lets you Doodle simple pieces together, one at a time and then combine them to make an intricate artistic Doodle.

Project #4: Pyramid Star

For this project, you're going to make a sculpture that can be hung as a mobile, or displayed on a table. In our example we have used ABS plastic, choosing a combination of light blue, dark blue and glow in the dark. You will also need a piece of paper, a pencil and a ruler.

1. In this project, you will make 24 equilateral triangles of the same size. Use your ruler to draw a few identical triangles with each side measuring two inches (about 5 cm).

   NOTE: An equilateral triangle is a triangle with sides of equal length.

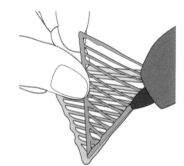

2. Trace over the triangles you have drawn and fill them in, as illustrated. You can use a side-to-side motion, cross-hatch or be creative – find a pattern that works for you!

3. Repeat until you have made 24 triangles. We suggest you make eight triangles in light blue ABS, eight in dark blue ABS and eight in glow in the dark ABS.

4. Next, assemble the triangles into eight pyramids. Each pyramid is made of three triangles with each side a different color. To weld the first two sides together, simply Doodle a straight line of plastic between them. The easiest way to weld the first two sides is to hold one triangle flat against a table or flat surface, as illustrated.

5. Repeat to weld the third side, forming a pyramid. The easiest way to do so is to stand the pyramid shape upright, as illustrated.

   Repeat until you have made all eight pyramids.

6. Next, you will create two structures each made from four pyramids. Avoid having two sides of the same color next to each other. To make the first structure, lay two pyramids on their sides and weld them together along their edges.

7. One by one, attach two more pyramids to the two you welded in step 6. Be sure that the open side with no plastic is always facing inward. It should look like the illustration.

8. Repeat steps 6 and 7 until you have created a second structure, the same as the first.

9. Now, it's time to join the two structures together. Note that the middle of each structure is an empty square shape. To weld the structures, Doodle some plastic on each corner of the squares, as illustrated and stick the structures together.

10. To strengthen the piece and fill in any gaps, Doodle a continuous line around the middle of the sculpture. Doodle more plastic into any gaps, as needed.

You've just made your first Doodled sculpture!

TIP: Why not pass a thread through one of the corners of your sculpture and hang it? You could even try making more, from different colors, to make a cluster of pyramid stars!

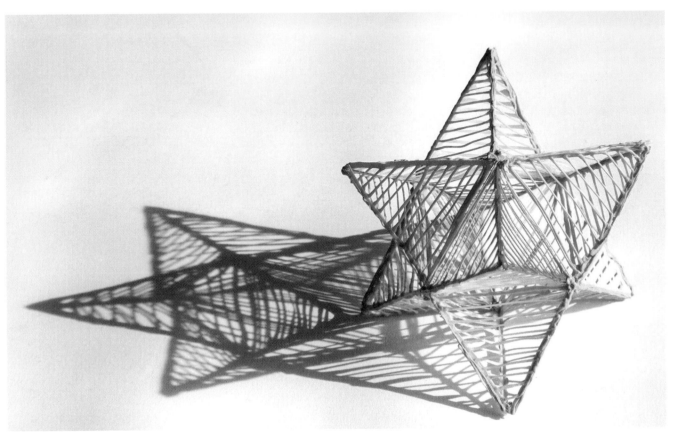

Marie Rouillon

Fashion is all about expressing yourself – wearing something that highlights your personal style. With the 3Doodler, you don't have to shop for that special accessory – you can make it!

Project #5: Headband

A good place to start is with simple items like rings, bracelets, necklaces, or in the case of this tutorial – a headband. Later, you can try to create your own more complex items!

The center piece of the headband is a flower, made from PLA. And to tie the band around your head, you'll Doodle a band with FLEXY plastic.

For this project you will need PLA, FLEXY, a pair of scissors, card or construction paper – something that is thick enough to hold a slight curve, like a real petal would have, double-sided tape and black masking tape.

NOTE: When making bracelets, rings – or anything – do not Doodle on your skin.

Making the flower

1. First, you will make the flower that forms the center of the headband. The flower is made from three differently sized layers of petals, with the biggest petals as the bottom layer and the smallest as the top. You will make a total of 14 petals.

2. Cut a piece of card or construction paper and cut five petal shapes for the largest, bottom row. About two inches (5 cm) is a good size but if you are making it for a smaller child, you might want to try a slightly smaller size or the flower will be too big on the child's head.

3. Bend the paper petals so they are curved like a real petal. Using PLA of any color, Doodle a line up the center of your petal and then remove it. It should look like a rib and will from the 'skeleton' of your petal. Doodle four more rib lines up the center of the petal, until you have five in total.

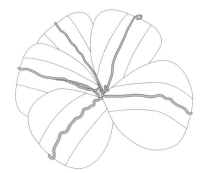

4. Stick the five paper petals together, so that they look like a flower. They do not need to meet in the center – it is your armature and doesn't need to be perfect.

5. Next, stick a strip of double-sided tape along the middle of each paper petal and stick the rib lines in place. Doodle a grid over the paper petal, incorporating the rib line. Repeat until all five petals have been Doodled. Allow the center of the Doodled petals to join together with the plastic. Carefully remove the paper. You now have the bottom layer of larger petals.

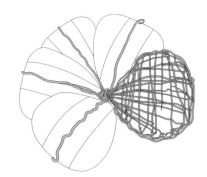

6. Repeat steps 1 and 2 to create five petals for the middle layer of the flower, but be sure to make the petals a bit smaller, around 1.5 inches (4 cm) in size. You can stick the paper petals onto the bottom layer of already Doodled petals, so they have a similar curve.

7. Attach the petals together at the center but be sure not to attach the two layers of petals together yet.

8. Repeat steps 1 and 3, making just four even smaller petals, around one inch (2.5 cm) in size. Now you have three different layers of petals ranging from small to medium and large.

9. Load a new color into your pen and Doodle a decorative flourish on the top of each of the petals, however you want to. Be creative!

10. Now that your petals are decorated, it's time to put them together to create a single flower. Use the heat of the nozzle to weld the different layers together: First, weld the middle, medium-sized petal row inside the bottom, larger row. Finally, weld the top, smaller row of petals into the center at the top.

Bo Lau

Making the headband

1. The headband will be made from three strips of FLEXY, braided together.

2. Doodle a single line about 30 inches (76 cm) long, then Doodle four more lines side-by-side to make a single, stronger, wide line.

3. Repeat two more times, creating three single, strong wide lines (each comprised of five lines), which will be braided together.

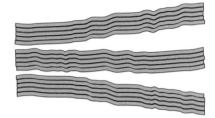

4. Weld them together at one end and tape the sealed end to a flat surface and then braid them together. When you have finished, weld the open end together, to create a single, long braid.

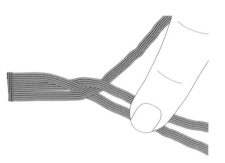

5. Now it's time to weld the flower with the braid. Using PLA, Doodle another flat band of plastic that is five lines thick and about six inches (15 cm) long. Attach the middle of it to the bottom of your flower.

6. Hold the band of plastic with flower attached against the braided band and weld them together using black PLA. Now your headband is ready for you to tie on and wear!

Well done, you've just joined a series of professional designers and fashionistas who have been using the 3Doodler to make dresses, hats, jewelry, purses – there's even a wearable 3Doodler jacket!

TIP: Not sure how to braid? It's the same as when you braid hair. Look for videos online to show you how!

Bo Lau

Louis DeRosa

The 3Doodler creates a textured look because everything is made from strands of extruded plastic. While it's a unique style, it makes natural objects look especially good.

Project #6: Tree

In this project, we're going to make a tree – and after that you could make a whole forest using the techniques here. We suggest PLA plastic for this project because it's malleable when cooling and will allow you to re-shape the branches by hand. A pair of scissors might be useful for trimming unwieldy branches.

1. First, Doodle the roots of the tree by Doodling the outline of the tree roots, as illustrated. Be sure they are wide enough to support the tree. Add a second layer of plastic, to create a strong foundation.

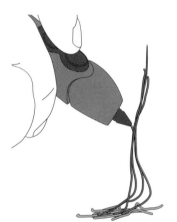

2. Next, create the core of the lower part of the trunk. Pressing gently against the center of the base, draw upward to make a single vertical line of plastic until you are satisfied with the height. Repeat this step four or five times and pinch the vertical lines together with your fingers.

   NOTE: Don't go too high – you will Doodle the top of the tree later!

3. Now, make the lower trunk stronger. Start a new flow of plastic and attach it to the base by pressing gently. Then, Doodle a coil around the vertical lines you just made, by working up to the top and then back down to the base before cutting the flow. Now you have a sturdy lower trunk.

4. It's time to Doodle the branches. About halfway up the lower trunk, gently press the pen into the side of the tree and start the flow. Doodle a tight coil on the side of the trunk, as illustrated. Be sure it's not too long, or your tree might fall over!

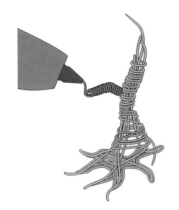

5. Add more branches, by following step 4. It's best to work your way around the trunk so you can be sure the tree is balanced.

    To make the branches look real, they need to be thinner towards the tip. Gently press the pen against the end of a branch coil and Doodle a single line outward. Repeat this with the other branch coils.

    Why not be creative and make them at different angles? But, always be sure to balance the branches, so the tree is stable.

6. Now that the lower part of the tree has a strong foundation and good balance, you can make it taller by Doodling a vertical coil up from the top of the lower trunk (which you have already made). You can coil up until the tree is almost double its current height. To finish, straighten your line and make the very top a single line of plastic.

7. If your tree feels steady, add a few more thin branches to the upper trunk. You can use your hands to adjust them into the shapes you want before the plastic is finished cooling.

Great work! Now you've made one tree, why not make a forest? Try different sizes, shapes or colors!

TIP: Vary the size and shape of the branches to imitate the natural variation in a real tree! Are a few of your branches too long? Use scissors to trim them!

Erin Song

With the excitement of drawing in mid-air, Doodlers sometimes forget that they can still use the 3Doodler like a regular pen. And when you do, the results are anything but ordinary!

Project #7: Portraits

Line drawings are one of the simplest things to Doodle – and portraits are a great place to start. You can Doodle over a photo of your subject, but be sure to make an extra copy before you trace over the lines in case you damage it. It's that simple!

You will need a copy of the portrait you want to make, PLA plastic and if you have the 3Doodler Nozzle Set, the 0.5mm nozzle works best for this project.

1. First, Doodle over the outline of your subject. That is, Doodle the shoulders, the outline of the clothing, hair, head, face and where the hair meets the face. These lines can be thicker to make a stronger structure.

2. Fill in the details, like the lines in the clothing, features of the face and the fine lines. Be sure not to overdo the lines in the face, or your subject may look older than they are! Too much detail can also make it harder to tell who the person is.

    NOTE: You need to plan where the features of the face will attach to the outline you Doodled in step 1 and draw them as one solid, uninterrupted Doodle because it needs to be one single piece, overall. Or, you can Doodle the main parts and attach them with Clearly Clear PLA. If your Doodle's facial features are breaking off, you can reattach them to the outline with clear PLA, which will not be very noticeable.

3. When you have finished the face, fill in the detailed lines of the hair and shade in any clothing, as you want. Use different colors and experiment with different types of lines and textures for the hair.

Erin Song

Well done Da Vinci! You are truly becoming an accomplished Doodler.

Using the basic method here, you can create and recreate any image you want, whether drawings, paintings, pictures of celebrities, or photos of your family and friends. A 3Doodled portrait makes a great gift!

TIP: The pen may damage your original portrait, so we suggest using a copy of it. Since you are doing fine line work, we advise that you tape over the picture with masking tape because it will peel off more easily, keeping your delicate Doodle intact.

Marie Rouillon

By now, you're getting to know the 3Doodler – and just how complex your creations can get!

Project #8: Bird

In this project, you're going to make a life-size bird. To create the bird, you'll first Doodle the body, by creating an armature (an armature is a frame on which you can build something) in the shape of a bird. Then, you'll cover it with feathers, wings and a beak to create the finished bird.

You will need scissors and you can use either ABS or PLA for this, but we recommend ABS because it will cool faster and create a sturdier 3D armature inside the bird, which you will attach the feathers to.

You will need the stencil provided here to make the bird. We suggest you photocopy it, or download it from the website and then cover it in masking tape to form your Doodling surface. PLA and other plastics will stick easily to paper.

Find stencils at
the3Doodler.com/create/

1. Follow the stencil to start Doodling the armature for your bird. Fill the outline with a few diagonal lines, creating a flat but sturdy grid – this is the internal armature of the bird – so don't worry about making it pretty.

2. Now it's time to give the bird a fuller body: Working on one side of the body at a time, draw lines upward. To do so, lay your Doodle flat and draw a line about one inch (2.5 cm) tall, starting on the grid you created in step 1. Repeat every 0.5 inches (about 1 cm).

    Gently turn over the armature and repeat to create the other side of its body. Once you have built up the bulk of the body, start forming the profile shape of a bird, as in the illustration.

    Once you have finished, carefully trim with scissors to create the details in the shape you want.

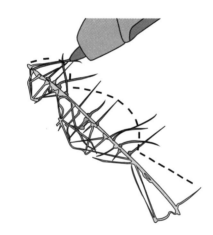

3. Next, create a finished body by joining the lines (created in step 2) together, to add a surface to the armature. First, be sure that you have trimmed them and are happy with the overall shape – or trim more as you go, if need be.

    To join the lines, Doodle around the armature, linking each of the lines together. Keep building until you're satisfied with the shape and have a dense network of criss-cross plastic. Don't be discouraged if it seems difficult at first – you don't have to be precise and every bird will be different.

4. It's time to make the feathers. Using the stencil provided, start with the smaller feathers, Doodling the outline of a single feather and then filling it in, using a side-to-side motion to create texture. The number of feathers needed will vary depending on the size of your bird, so we suggest creating a batch of ten to twenty first, then attaching them, to indicate how many you might need.

5. Weld the feathers to the bird's body with the pen. To give a natural look, start at the end of the tail, working from left to center and when done, work from right to center. Attach the central-most feather last.

6. After you have finished the first row, follow the same routine to make the second row, attaching the next row slightly above the first, to create a natural look.

7. Repeat row by row, moving upward, until you have covered the lower half of the bird's body with feathers. Stop when you reach the area where the wings will be attached, as you'll need to attach the wings before putting the rest of the feathers on the body.

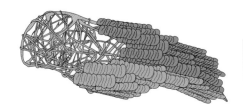

8. To make the longer wing feathers (we've used silver in the finised piece on page 41), follow the stencil provided. When done, Doodle the feathers together one by one, slightly overlapping them to create a natural look. Refer to the stencil to be sure that you are crafting a nice, curved wing.

9. The shorter, overlapping feathers (we've used purple in the finised piece on page 41) are a similar size to the feathers used on the body. Note that there are three layers to this part of the wing and you might want to make slightly smaller feathers for the base of the wings, closest to the body.

10. After you have Doodled the individual feathers, weld the feathers together one-by-one to create a layer of feathers, slightly overlapping them for a natural look.

11. Once each row is made, weld the rows together, with the feathers at the base of the wings positioned closest to the body on top and the feathers closest to the inner wings on the bottom, as illustrated.

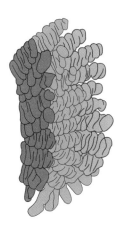

12. Now you can carefully weld the longer and shorter wing pieces to create a full wing.

13. Attach the wings to the armature on the upper body, one by one, welding them in the position. To do so, Doodle some plastic between the wing and the armature, holding the wing in place with your non-Doodling hand. Do the same on the underside of the wing, to make it sturdy.

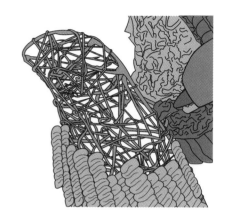

14. Once the wings are attached, cover the rest of the body with feathers. Follow steps 4 to 6 until the entire body is covered.

15. Now, it's time to make the beak, which consists of four triangle shapes. Choose your color – which will later form the eyes, too – then Doodle four triangles on a flat Doodling surface. To create a smooth beak, cut the triangles so that they are the exact same shape and then turn them over, so that the smooth side, which was against the Doodle surface, is on the outside of the beak.

16. To weld them together, place one triangle on a flat surface. Hold a second triangle at a 90° angle and weld the two triangles together. Repeat with the other two triangles, so that you have two half pyramids – and then weld the two halves together. Fill in any noticeable gaps on the outside with plastic.

17. Finally, attach the beak and draw the eyes. To do so, attach the beak to the bird's head with a little plastic on either side. As you attach the beak, draw upward onto the head and form a circle, on each side of the head. Finish it with another color, if you want to draw pupils.

Well done! Was that as hard as it looked? Now it's time to make a cage, or your bird might fly away!

TIP: Why not play with colors, by using a different color for the top and underside of the body?

Body

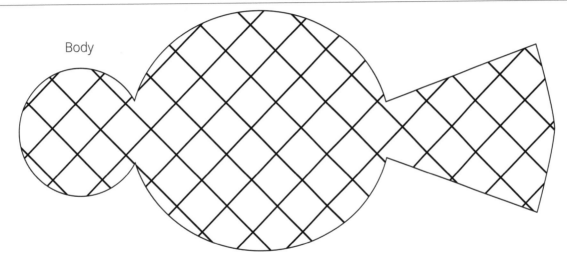

Feathers

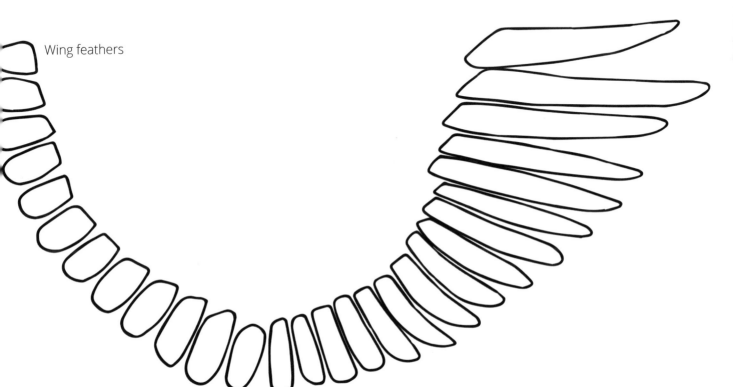

S

Wing feathers

Marie Rouillon

PROJECT #8: BIRD & BIRDCAGE

Birdcages make a great ornament – even without a bird inside!

Birdcage

First, you'll create the dome of the cage using the stencils provided and a balled up piece of tissue paper, then you will Doodle a grid on a flat surface and bend the plastic to make the main body of the cage.

To prepare, you'll need some scissors, a sheet of paper, a balled up piece of tissue paper and there's an option to use an iron.

The stencil is included and we suggest you photocopy it, or download it from the website and then cover it in masking tape to form your Doodling surface. PLA and other plastics will stick easily to paper.

Find stencils at
the3Doodler.com/create/

Making the base

1. First, make the base of the cage. To do so, Doodle over the circle in the stencil provided.

2. Beading up some plastic at the edge of the circle to anchor the plastic firmly, Doodle a line across the circle. Repeat, creating a grid of lines, as illustrated.

   When finished, Doodle over the outside of the circle again to strengthen it and firmly attach each line of your grid. Now you have completed the base of the cage.

   If it isn't flat enough, you can use a warm iron to flatten it. To do so, place the circle between two sheets of greaseproof paper, place it on an ironing board and press down gently with the iron on medium heat. Don't move the iron around, just press on it for a few seconds.

Making the dome

1. Next, make the dome at the top of the birdcage. To do so, Doodle over the two circles in the provided stencil. Use a balled up piece of tissue paper to create a mold for the dome shape, with the larger circle at the bottom (on top of your Doodling surface) and the smaller circle at the top.

2. Starting from the larger circle, which is against your Doodling surface, anchor some plastic and draw a line upward to the smaller circle and anchor the plastic. Repeat this every 0.5 inches (about 1 cm), going around the balled up paper, Doodling single upward lines, creating a dome. Then, remove the balled up paper from inside the dome.

3. Doodle another small circle using the provided stencil then repeat step 2 to Doodle a grid onto it. This is the top of your dome.

4. Place the dome the correct way up and use the heat of your pen and a little plastic to weld the top of the dome to the body of the dome, as illustrated.

Making the main cage

Here, we recommend ABS because it is more pliable.

1. Using the stencil, Doodle the outer rectangle, first.

2. Doodle the straight lines that fill the rectangle and include the little square door shape, following the stencil. You can ignore the decorative diagonal lines if you want to.

3. Doodle over the top and bottom edges of the rectangle again, to make sure the straight lines are firmly attached. Neaten it by cutting off any excess plastic.

4. Pull the main cage rectangle off the stencil and bend it into a cylinder shape. Use the pen to weld it to the base you made in step 2. It is easiest to do so by having the base at the top, closest to you. Be sure to Doodle extra plastic over the outside of the circle a few times so it is firmly held together and weld the meeting ends of the rectangle together.

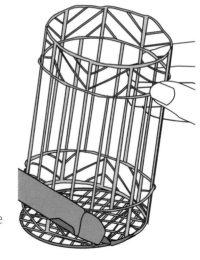

5. Now, use the pen to seal the top of the dome against the circular body. Be sure to Doodle extra plastic over the outside of the circle a few times so it is firmly held together.

    NOTE: If you want to put your bird inside – or anything else – do so before sealing the dome.

Wow, now you have your own bird cage Doodle!

TIP: You can add decorative elements at the top and bottom of the cage. Try Doodling them while the cage is still flat. Be creative!

TIP: To make a cage with a door that can open, cut the door out of the main rectangle. Then, Doodle two small loops and weld them to the side of the door that you have cut out. These will be the hinges.

On the main rectangle, cut the top of the vertical line where you will attach the door back onto the main rectangle – this is the door frame line. Slide the door onto the frame line by its hinge loops. Then, reattach the top of the door frame to the main rectangle by welding it with some plastic. If your door slides down the door frame line, Doodle a little ledge under one of the hinge loops, to keep it from sliding down.

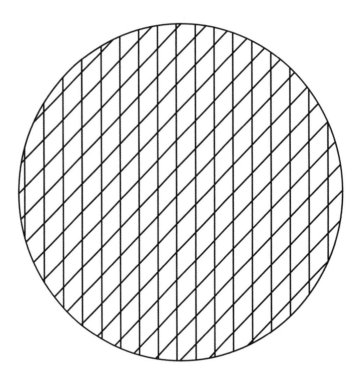

S

Like with photography and social media, food seems to be a favorite among the 3Doodler community. And food is ideal because you can make it life-sized without using too much plastic – and it's great fun to showcase the wide range of colors that make Doodles look so real!

WARNING: This project will make you hungry!

Project #9: Hamburger

You're going to make a hamburger, by Doodling each ingredient separately before stacking it together, just like when you make a real burger! You will need a ruler and a balled up piece of tissue paper.

The stencil is included and we suggest you photocopy it, or download it from the website and then cover it in masking tape to form your Doodling surface. PLA and other plastics will stick easily to paper.

Find stencils at
the3Doodler.com/create/

Making the bun

1. Start by making the bun using a tan or light brown plastic. First Doodle a circle and then Doodle criss-cross lines inside the circle, creating a strong grid before shading it in, over the grid – as illustrated. This will be the base of your bottom bun.

2. Now, trace two more circles and Doodle a grid inside, but do not fill them in. Put one circle aside for now and join the other with side of the bun you made in step 1.

    To do so, lay the shaded circle made in step 1 on a flat surface and then anchor and bead up some plastic on the edge of it. Doodle a line straight up, about 0.4 inches (1 cm) high. Doodle more lines around the edge of the shaded circle about every 0.5 inches (1 cm).

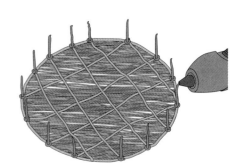

3. Attach the other circle to the top of the vertical lines by welding them with plastic.

4. Using a continuous flow, anchor your plastic to the perimeter of the circle and wrap the line around the edge of the bun until the sides are solid, as illustrated.

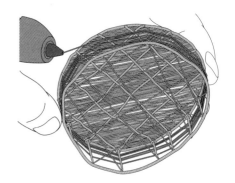

5. Put the bottom bun aside, for now. It's time to start the top bun, so there is no need to change plastic. Take the circle with the grid which you set aside in step 2 and anchor some plastic to the edge. Then, Doodle an arch up over the circle, free hand and weld the plastic on the other side of the circle, as illustrated. Repeat until you have created the rough shape of a dome, which will form the top bun.

   NOTE: If you find it difficult to Doodle free hand, try Doodling over a balled up piece of tissue paper, like you did for the dome for the birdcage on page 48.

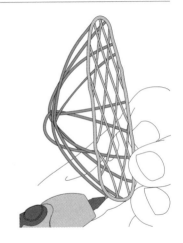

6. Now, fill in the top, so it's solid.

7. Switch to white plastic and draw some sesame seeds on the top of your bun, if you want to. Then, shade in the flat underside of the top bun, and the top side of your bottom bun.

Making the patty and other ingredients

1. Now it's time to make the burger patty. Load the pen with dark brown ABS and Doodle two more gridded circles, a tiny bit smaller than the ones you made for the bun.

2. Join the two sides together, by first drawing a line up from one circle, like you did in the second part of step 2 and then follow step 3 to weld the sides together.

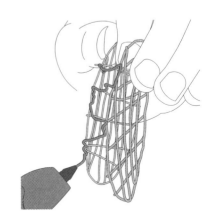

3. Make the burger patty solid by wrapping the armature you made in step 2 with plastic. To do so, anchor a line of plastic to the edge and wrap extruded plastic around it, trying not to break the flow of plastic.

   This is great practice for perfecting the relationship between your wrist and hand movements and the flow of plastic, (extrusion speed).

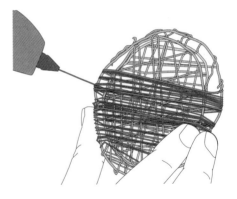

4. Want a cheeseburger? Doodle a slice of cheese with translucent orange or yellow PLA. Simply Doodle a square and fill it in, then layer it up a few times. You might want to try cross-hatching.

5. Like tomatoes? Doodle a tomato with red ABS. Make two, following the stencil provided.

   To do so, start with the circular outer edge and core. Then, change to translucent red PLA and shade in the area between the outer edge and core, making it thinner than the outer edge. Change to translucent yellow PLA and Doodle some seeds.

6. Like a crunch? Use translucent green PLA to Doodle about twelve narrow strips about two inches (6 cm) long. Bend them a bit with your fingers so they have a bit of curve to them, like real shredded lettuce. If you weld them together they will stay in place more easily.

7. Stack up your Doodled ingredients to make a cheeseburger!

Great work, chef – you're really cooking now! Like food, Doodles sometimes take time to prepare. Bon appetit!

TIP: Decide whether you want to keep your cheeseburger separate and loose, or use a little plastic to weld them all together.

Louis DeRosa

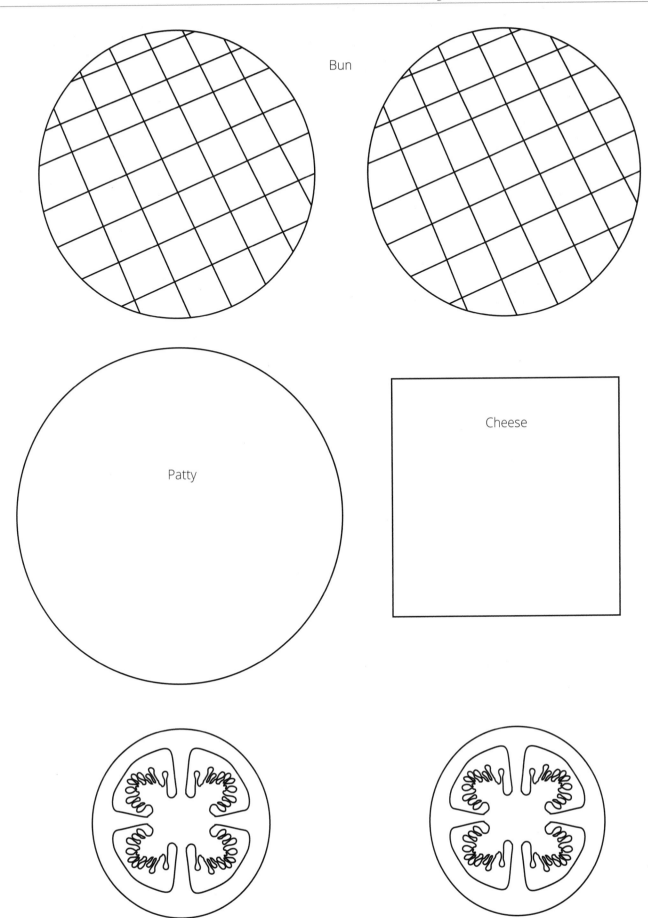

Bun

Patty

Cheese

PROJECT #10: DRAGON

Combining stencil work with free hand Doodling is good practice and very effective – you can create really life-like Doodles!

Project #10: Dragon

In this project you'll hone your skills by making a majestic dragon that stands on its own feet and spreads its wings. To make the dragon, you might choose to use several different plastics and a pair of scissors might be useful.

You will need the stencil provided here to make the dragon. We suggest you photocopy it, or download it from the website and then cover it in masking tape to form your Doodling surface. PLA and other plastics will stick easily to paper.

Find stencils at
the3Doodler.com/create/

1. The dragon's spine and body are the starting point for this piece. Trace the outline of the stencil and then fill it in.

2. Carefully peel the Doodle off the stencil or Doodling surface. Then Doodle the body, building it up by Doodling layers and creating a more rounded shape on top of the part you made in step 1. A rounded ribcage, narrow waist and wider hindquarters will look good.

3. Using the stencil, Doodle the feet. As you make each one, coil upwards free hand, to create a leg. Repeat three times to make the remaining feet and legs.

4. Weld the legs to the body at the points indicated on the stencil. If the dragon is unstable you can either add more plastic to the feet to stabilize it or trim the leg by cutting it with scissors.

5. It's time to make the dragon's head. Trace the stencil and then layer the head until it looks like a dragon's head with a snout. You can then Doodle a small horn on the tip of the snout and two bigger horns, rising up from the dragon's brow. To make the jaw, trace the stencil again and layer up a couple of times until you have a flat jaw piece.

6. Attach the jaw to the head so that the dragon's mouth is open, as illustrated. Then weld the head to the neck.

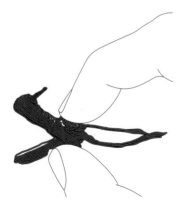

7. To make the wings, use the stencil. Doodle the outline in black and then shade them in, using a different color, if you want to. A side-to-side line looks good – and translucent plastic looks particularly cool!

8. Weld the wings to the body as incidated in the stencil. Be sure to Doodle some extra plastic around the shoulder and the base of the wing so that they are welded together firmly.

9. Now it's time to add some additional spikes along the back. Space them out evenly, to match the ones you Doodled in step 1.

10. Your dragon is complete. But if he is going to face fierce battle, you can can Doodle around the joins you made at the head, legs, feet and wings, to make him extra strong.

Now that is one fearsome dragon you just Doodled!

TIP: When layering up the body area, if you want to Doodle quickly, don't worry about the texture and flow of the lines until you get to the outside layer – the dragon can be messy on the inside but sleek on the outside!

TIP: To make the wings look even more realistic, you can use FLEXY and they will be more pliable!

TIP: If you want to personalize your dragon more, add scales or designs in different colors or add extra spikes. You can even use translucent red, yellow and orange to make fire come out of his mouth!

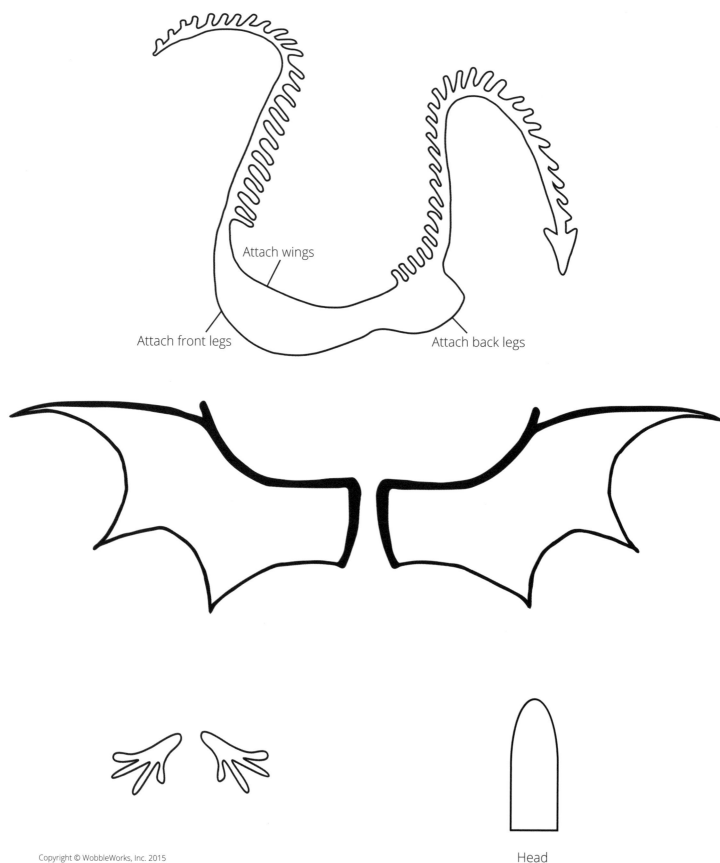

Attach wings

Attach front legs

Attach back legs

Head

Marisa Lewis

PROJECT #11: DINOSAUR

Doesn't everyone love dinosaurs? We do, so let's make a triceratops fossil!

Project #11: Dinosaur

Using the stencil provided you will create the bones and weld them together to make a free-standing durable triceratops skeleton. Use the plastic and color of your choice!

You will need the stencil provided here to make the dinosaur. We suggest you photocopy it, or download it from the website and then cover it in masking tape to form your Doodling surface. PLA and other plastics will stick easily to paper.

Find stencils at
the3Doodler.com/create/

1. Follow the stencil provided, to create the basic skeleton. To do so, first Doodle the outline, fill it in and then layer it up a bit.

2. Gently remove the pieces from your Doodling surface and layer up the flat underside so that they are even on both sides and have a rough, fossilized texture.

It's time to assemble your fossils! Follow the instructions below but be sure to refer to the image of the finished triceratops, so you attach each bone in the correct place.

1. First, weld the ribs onto the spine. Make sure the biggest rib is at the front and the smallest is toward the tail.

2. Join the pointy tip of the shoulder blades together, then attach the other ends to the outside of the rib cage, where the shoulders should be.

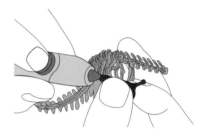

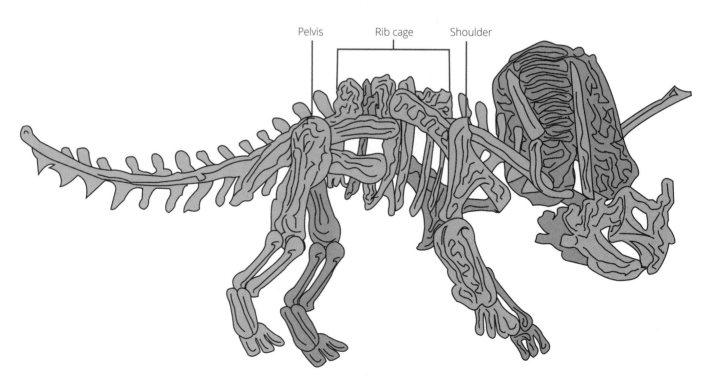

Pelvis   Rib cage   Shoulder

3. One by one, weld the pelvic bones to the sides of the spine, near the back of the rib cage but not behind the rib cage.

4. Attach the legs to the outside of the pelvic bones, as illustrated on the opposite page. Be sure to check that the feet are are even and that the dinosuar can stand. To do so, you might need to slightly adjust the angle at which each leg is attached.

5. It's time to assemble the skull. To do so, hold both sides of the skull slightly apart at an angle but have the snout tips touch. Then Doodle the top of the skull by stringing plastic between the two sides, as illustrated.

6. Attach the shield bone (as labeled on the stencil) to the longest bone at the back of the skull just behind the horns. Be sure to weld the straight sides together – that is, the rounded edge of the shield bone should face outward. Doodle over all of the joins in the skull, including on the inside, to reinforce it.

7. It's time to assemble the lower jaw. To do so, hold both sides together at the front of the jaw, with the back ends slightly apart (like when you made the skull) and then weld them together.

8. Attach the lower jaw to the skull by carefully holding the skull and lower jaw together and welding them together through the opening at the back.

9. Attach the completed skull to the body, by holding it against the top of the spine and welding it together.

10. Doodle over all the joins to make a strong and tough triceratops – he might have to fight a T-Rex!

Doodling is far from prehistoric, but you've just Doodled a dinosaur!

TIP: When Doodling figures that stand, it's important to check the balance as you go. Finished Doodles that are wobbly can be fixed – choose from cutting a piece off and re-attaching it, trimming the bottom with scissors or beading up some extra plastic on the bottom to get the right balance.

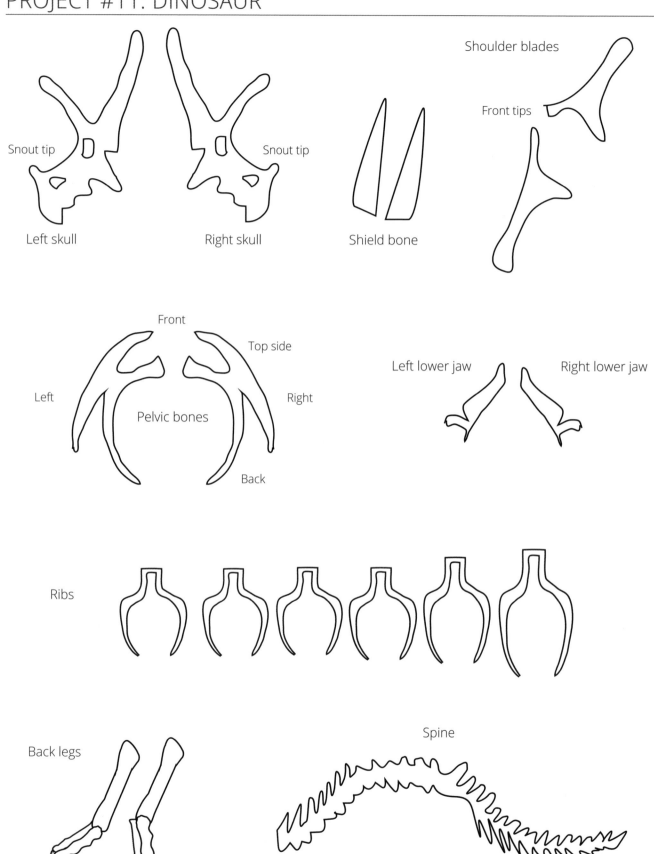

Snout tip

Snout tip

Shoulder blades

Front tips

Left skull

Right skull

Shield bone

Front

Top side

Left

Right

Pelvic bones

Back

Left lower jaw

Right lower jaw

Ribs

Spine

Back legs

Neck

Tail

Faraz Warsi

Marisa Lewis

PROJECT #12: WINDMILL

Creating buildings and structures from a stencil is a great way to create an impressive Doodle.

Project #12: Windmill

Doodling a grid of lines with your pen and attaching them to create a free standing Doodle is a bit like making a blueprint come to life! And this tutorial has techniques that are great for other architectural Doodles.

You're going to make a windmill, with a sail that spins! Use plastic either in a single color, or as many colors as you want. You will also need a pair of wire cutters or sharp scissors.

The stencil is included and we suggest you photocopy it, or download it from the website and then cover it in masking tape to form your Doodling surface. PLA and other plastics will stick easily to paper.

Find stencils at
the3Doodler.com/create/

1. Trace over the stencil provided, Doodling the tower, the ladder, sails, vane and platform. When you make the sails, be sure to layer up a few times, with a side to side motion.

   To make the gearbox, use the stencil to fill in the rectangles and then weld them together into a sturdy hollow box.

2. Gently lift the pieces from your Doodling surface and then weld the four pieces that form the tower together first. It's easiest to lay one piece flat at the edge of a table and hold the adjoining piece at a 90° angle while welding it with your Doodling hand.

3. Reinforce the welded corners of the tower with a line of plastic to make sure it is stable. Next, weld the ladder to the tower. Then, weld the platform to the top of the tower.

4. To make sails that spin, make an axle. Use a pair of wire cutters to cut a piece of an unused strand of plastic about two inches (5 cm) long and weld it to the back of the sails in the middle, as illustrated.

   Then take the gearbox you welded together in step 1. Use the heat of the nozzle to make a small hole at both ends of the gearbox. Push the axle all the way through the holes. Finally, weld the gearbox to the tower.

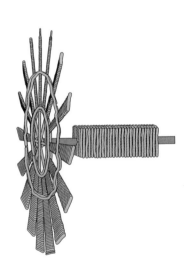

5. Weld the vane to the back of the axle with plastic.

Now that you have a windmill that spins, it's time to start generating renewable energy!

TIP: Whenever you need a stick or pole in a Doodle, you can use an unused strand of plastic.

Tower

Ladder

Vane

Gearbox

Platform

Sails

S

Animals are among the most popular Doodles to create. With so many to choose from, you can showcase your different Doodling methods and you can go from life-like to cartoon-like!

Project #13: Gorilla

You're going to make a gorilla, using a mixture of stencils and free hand work. You will need a drink can or similar shaped object, a hard-boiled egg covered in masking tape (or a balled up piece of tissue paper). We recommend black plastic for most of the body and you can add details in grey or white – or whatever color you want.

You will need the stencil provided here to make the gorilla. We suggest you photocopy it, or download it from the website and then cover it in masking tape to form your Doodling surface. PLA and other plastics will stick easily to paper.

Find stencils at
the3Doodler.com/create/

1. First, make the gorilla's head. Take a hard-boiled egg and cover it in masking tape (or use a balled up piece of tissue paper, without masking tape) and Doodle over the more pointed, top half of the egg, as illustrated. Remove the Doodle from the egg (or tissue paper) and repeat so that you have two half spheres.

2. Weld the two halves together to form the gorilla's head. Ours is about 1.5 inches (4 cm) across.

3. To make the body, repeat step 1, using the rounder bottom of the egg, again making two half spheres. Put them aside and do not weld them together.

4. Using a small drink can can or similarly shaped object, Doodle eight strips of plastic just under two inches (5 cm) long and about 0.5 inches (1.3 cm) wide. These will form the middle of the gorilla's body.

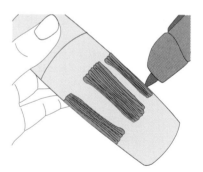

5. Take one of the larger half spheres made in step 3 and weld the strips of plastic to it, as illustrated. Then weld the other half sphere (made in step 3) to the other end of the plastic strips, creating a long body. Ours is about 2.25 inches (6 cm) in total. Fill in any gaps with the pen.

6. To make the hips, free hand Doodle a small dome rising up from one end of the body. The dome should be 0.75 inches (2 cm) high but narrower than the rest of the body. It is easiest to Doodle a rough armature onto the body and then layer it up. Later, you will attach the legs here.

7. To Doodle the gorilla's arms and legs, use the stencil provided. Be sure to layer them up so they are rounded, like a gorilla's limbs.

8. Weld the arms and legs to the body.

9. Use the stencil provided to Doodle the hands and feet – we've used grey. Be sure to layer up the top side, but the undersides should remain flat so your gorilla is stable when it stands.

    Weld the hands and feet to the body. Be sure the gorilla can stand.

10. Doodle some grey plastic on the chest to create the distinctive fur pattern that gorillas are known for, as illustrated.

11. Now it's time to Doodle the face. Take the head that you made in step 1 and Doodle the outline of the face by Doodling a single line for each feature before building it up.

12. Doodle the brow, cheeks and chin, then build out the bulge of the big round nostrils and mouth, with the upper lip sticking out further than the lower one. Keep Doodling until you have the face that you want!

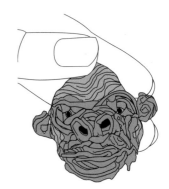

13. You'll need black plastic to finish the gorilla's face: Give him black eyes, nostrils and a line for his mouth.

14. Now, weld the head to the body by coiling a short, thick neck on top of the body and then welding the head to the top of the neck with the 3Doodler.

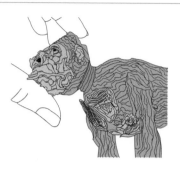

Tired of monkeying around? You can use the methods in this project to make almost any animal you can think of. Why not Doodle some friends for your gorilla?

TIP: If you are not satisfied with the gorilla's face, you can melt the plastic with the heat of the 3Doodler's nozzle and reshape it. While no two gorilla Doodles look the same, combining free hand Doodling with stencils creates unique pieces!

TIP: If you have the nozzle set, use the extra fine nozzle for the detailing work on the gorilla's face.

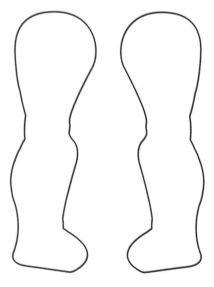

Legs

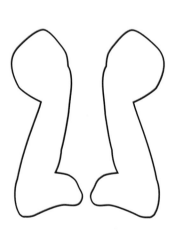

Arms

Hands & feet

Edith Shek

With the 3Doodler, you can really let your imgination fly!

Project #14: Airplane

That's right, you're going to use your 3Doodler to make an airplane!

For this project you will need ABS or PLA. Choose any color you want! You will also need a pair of scissors and you have the option of using an iron, like in the birdcage project.

The stencil is included and we suggest you photocopy it, or download it from the website and then cover it in masking tape to form your Doodling surface. PLA and other plastics will stick easily to paper.

Find stencils at
the3Doodler.com/create/

1. Start by filling in all parts of the stencil and layer up so that the airplane is sturdy. You can make the plane in a single color, or use two different ones for the body, to personalize it. For the wheels, it's best to use black and for the propeller and wheel supports (labeled in the stencil) it's best to use silver.

2. Peel your Doodles off your Doodling surface. If they are not flat enough, place them between two sheets of greaseproof paper and press them gently for a few seconds, with an iron on medium heat. Then begin to assemble the pieces with the smooth sides which were against the Doodling surface facing out.

3. Put the wing upside down and weld the two sides of the body to it. To do so, angle the two sides with a gap of about one inch (2.5 cm) between them at the nose and the tips touching, at the tail.

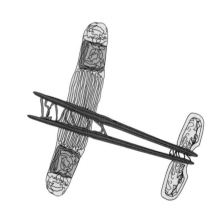

4. String some plastic back and forth between the two sides of the body to create the underside of the body as well as the nose (the front of the plane, on top). If any gaps remain when you are finished, fill them in and layer up, so that it looks even.

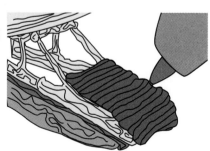

5.   Insert the horizontal stabilizer into the groove at the tail of the plane and weld it on, using the 3Doodler.

6.   Weld the vertical stabilizer, as labeled in the stencil, to the top of the plane.

7.   Weld the propeller to the nose of the plane and Doodle a little cone to mimic the hub at the center of the propeller, giving the plane a classic pointy nose.

8.   Weld the wheels to the end of the wheel supports.

9.   Lay the plane upside down on the edge of a table so that the vertical stabilizer doesn't get damaged and weld the wheel and wing supports, as illustrated. The shortest wheel support is the front wheel. You may have to adjust these to make sure the plane is stable when it's standing. If you have difficulties, cut them off and reattach.

10. Reinforce any weak spots and cut off any extra plastic.

Good work captain! Now, your plane is ready to fly – but you might not want to actually launch it through the air!

TIP: You don't have to vary the colors of the plastic you use when Doodling the plane to make it more realistic – you can wait until you are finished and decorate it with any color or design you want.

S

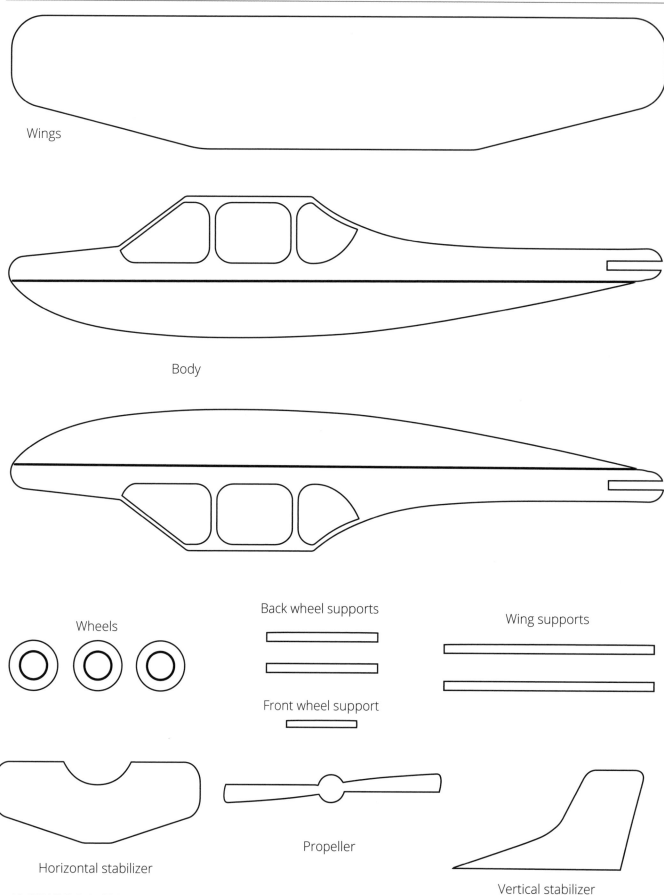

Wings

Body

Wheels

Back wheel supports

Front wheel support

Wing supports

Horizontal stabilizer

Propeller

Vertical stabilizer

Joe James

Greetings from
MOJAVE

SPRINGS

Nikka Francisco

There are endless possibilities for making figurines and little characters with the 3Doodler. You can free hand simple figures, or carefully design more complex Doodles and construct them one piece at a time.

Project #15: Bobblehead Cowboy

To explore this type of character making, you are going to Doodle a bobblehead cowboy. For this project, you will need a few pieces of balled up tissue paper and a pair of wire cutters. We've used PLA: Royal Blue, Snow White, Brownie Brown, Café au Lait, Robo Silver, OJ Orange, Clearly Clear, Chili Pepper Red, Gangsta' Gold and Tuxedo Black – but use any colors you like.

The stencil is included and we suggest you photocopy it, or download it from the website and then cover it in masking tape to form your Doodling surface. PLA and other plastics will stick easily to paper.

Find stencils at
the3Doodler.com/create/

Will you make a crazy cowboy or a professional-looking hero who would make Billy the Kid run for the hills?

Making the body

1. Make the lower body, first – we've used Royal Blue. Follow the stencil to Doodle the waistline of the body. Then, place the Doodled waistline around the middle of the balled ball up a piece of tissue paper about two inches (5 cm) wide and fill out half of the sphere. Once you have a light layer, remove the tissue paper and layer up the half sphere.

2. To complete the lower body, coil the plastic to Doodle two legs coming down from the bottom of the half sphere. Finally, Doodle over the outside of the coils to give them a smoother surface that looks more like blue jeans, as illustrated.

3. Now make the upper body. Elongate your ball of paper so it is not a perfect sphere, but more like an egg. Doodle another half sphere (that's slightly elongated) – we've used Snow White. Be sure to leave holes for the neck and arms, as illustrated.

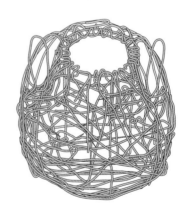

4. To make the upper arms, roll up a piece of paper about 1.5 cm wide or the width of a Sharpie marker pen and slide it through the armholes. Wind plastic around the paper until it looks like sleeves and weld the plastic onto the body – don't go too tight – once you have an armature for the sleeves, slide the paper out and then fill in the surface, as illlustrated.

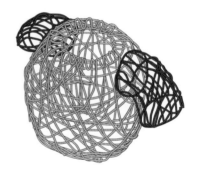

5. Weld the lower and upper body together firmly, as illlustrated.

6. To make the forearm, roll up a small piece of paper about 1.5 inches (4 cm) long but thinner than the roll from step 4, making sure it is tapered at one end – like a forearm. We used Cafe Au Lait to Doodle a one inch (2.5 cm) long coil around the paper, as illustrated. Repeat to make the second forearm.

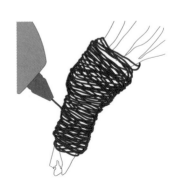

S

7. Slot the forearms inside the upper arms (or sleeve holes), angling them so that they hang at the cowboy's sides. Weld them on.

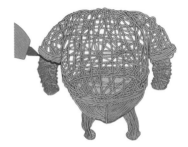

8. Doodle a wide thick belt around his waist – we've used Brownie Brown.

9. Now make his hand. Doodle a ball on the end of one of the forearms and add fingers if you want! Our cowboy is quite cartoon-like, but make yours how you want. Repeat to make the other hand.

10. To Doodle the boots, stand the cowboy up on your Doodling surface and weld some Robo Silver to the bottom of one of his legs, Doodling outward until you have created a boot shape, as illustrated.

    You can make any type of boot you like, but we made cowboy style boots. Layer up over the toe and heel of the boot, then Doodle a small coil around his lower leg, welding the boot to the leg, firmly. Repeat on the other side.

    NOTE: You will make a base around his feet later, so he doesn't have to be perfectly stable.

Making the head

1. To make the head, Doodle the outline of the face using the stencil – we've used Cafe au Lait.

    Make the nose stick out by placing a ball of paper on the tip of the nose and Doodling around it, giving the cowboy a bulbous nose. Then Doodle the bridge of the nose going back toward the brow. Then, layer up the brow ridges.

    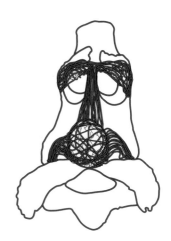

    NOTE: You don't need to remove the paper from under the nose until you remove the face from the stencil.

2. Fill in the rest of the face, making it as flat or textured as you want. We've used Brownie Brown for the mustache and eyebrows and Snow White for the whites of the eyes. Choose your favorite color for his pupils and a flesh tone for his lip.

3. Gently lift the face from the stencil and remove the ball of paper from inside the nose.

4. To complete his head, Doodle the neck and shoulders circle marked on the stencil, which will form the base of his head. Remove the circle from the stencil and weld it to the bottom of his face at a right angle. Next, Doodle the sides of the face by stringing lines from the sides of the circle to the top of the face, as illustrated.

    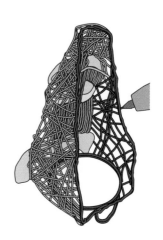

5. To make the back of the head, take a balled up piece of tissue paper and stuff it into the bottom of the head, making sure it fits comfortably with the parts you have already Doodled. Doodle over the balled up tissue paper, to make an armature. Gently remove the paper and layer up the rest of the head, leaving the top of the head open.

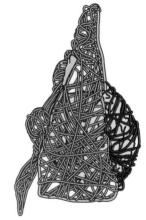

6. On the underside of the head, create a grid inside the circle you welded in step 4 and Doodle a smaller circle inside, as illustrated.

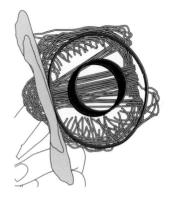

7. Use the stencil to create the outline of the ears. Weld them to the head. Fill them in by layering them up until they have a full, rounded shape, as illustrated.

S

8. It's time to cover the head with the hat – we've used OJ Orange. Using the stencil, Doodle the brim and then weld it to the top of the head at a slight angle so that you are covering the open space on the back of the head. The opening in the brim should be at the back of the head.

    NOTE: Don't fill in the hat completely, yet.

9. To create the crown of the hat, you will need a balled up piece of tissue paper about the same width as the inside of the hat's brim. Doodle over it until you have an armature in the shape of the crown of the hat – so that it has the classic cowboy hat shape – leaving the underside open. Remove the paper through the opening on the underside of the crown and then weld the armature of the crown to the brim of the hat.

10. Layer up the crown of the hat until it is solid, like a cowboy hat. The peak of the hat should come up above the face and you can create the little indents on the front by pinching them in as the plastic is setting. Finally, Doodle the band of the hat, as illustrated. We've used Brownie Brown.

11. Give your cowboy some hair coming out from under the brim of his hat at the front.

12. Now, it's time to add the details! We've added black shirt pockets, black fold lines around his shirt sleeves and stitching on his boots. We've made a neckerchief in Chili Pepper Red and used Gangsta' Gold to make a star over his front pocket and a belt buckle for his belt.

13. The Doodle is top heavy and needs a base so that it can stand. Using Clearly Clear PLA, Doodle a wide, flat base and weld the feet to the base, making sure they are firmly attached to it by Doodling over and around them a few times.

14. There's one thing missing – his head isn't yet attached to his body! Take a strand of unused plastic, trimming it with a pair of wire cutters to make the right length for your Doodle, and place it inside the body – it will lodge into his leg area. Then, place his head on the top end of the strand and it should balance, in a bobbly manner!

That was a tough one – and you did great! You'll be herding cows in no time at all.

TIP: If you want to, you can weld the head to the body with FLEXY.

TIP: Making intricate figures is easier when you make the body parts separately and then weld them together with the 3Doodler.

TIP: PLA is useful when welding parts together because it is strong and you have a little time to bend the Doodles into the shapes that best fit each other, before the plastic sets.

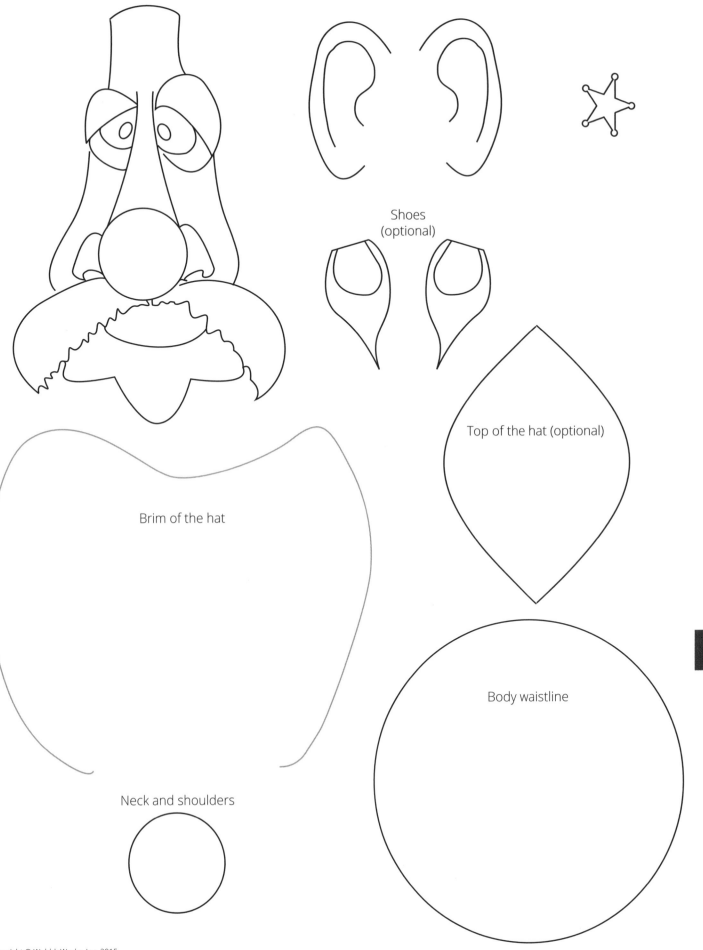

Shoes
(optional)

Top of the hat (optional)

Brim of the hat

Neck and shoulders

Body waistline

S

Action figures are always popular, so how about making one of your own? In this project you will learn how to make articulated joints that bend. Imagine what else you could make and how much fun you could have with your articulated Doodles!

Project #16: Articulated Action Figure

First, you will make the articulated joints, then you will connect them into the shape of a body. Next, you will Doodle the limbs and extremities, welding them to the body and layering up to make the figure solid. Finally, you will personalize your figure with a design of your choosing.

You will need wire cutters, ABS plastic and a 3 mm thick wire or any metal rod the same diameter as 3Doodler plastic strands, like a plain wire hanger. The wire will be easiest to use if it is at least six inches (15 cm) long.

NOTE: Use any color you like. The first steps are for making the basic armature of the figure, so you can use up leftover plastic and colors you don't use as often. Then, layer up the exterior with the colors you love.

Making the joints

Each joint is made of two parts: An axle and a socket.

1. To begin, you will make a socket. Doodle the outline of a little rectangle about 0.5 inches (1.25 cm) long and no more than 0.25 inches (0.6 cm) wide. Fill it in and layer it up. Then, press a piece of 3 mm thick wire across the middle of the rectangle, that is, perpendicular to the long sides of the rectangle, as illustrated, then Doodle over the wire and layer up the rectangle on both sides until the plastic is the height of the wire.

   Gently ease the wire out. If it sticks, be firm but gentle and don't worry if you crack the plastic – you can fix it later.

2. Take a new strand of plastic in a different color than you used to make the socket piece in step 1 and use a pair of wire cutters to cut off 0.5 inches (1.25 cm). This will be the axle. Slide the plastic strand through the hole in the socket you made in step 1. Inserting the plastic rod might cause the socket to crack. If so, Doodle over the crack to fix it.

3. Doodle a cap on each end of the axle, as illustrated, so that it cannot fall out of the socket piece. Later, you will Doodle an arm onto the cap.

   NOTE: Always check your joints to make sure they spin properly as you go and are not too tight or too loose.

   You now have your first shoulder joint. Repeat steps 1 to 3 to create the second shoulder joint.

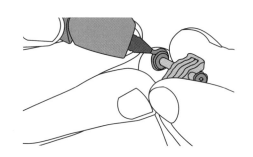

4. The pelvis and hip joints are made from three sockets on a single axle. To make them, repeat step 1, three times, making three new sockets. Then, cut an unused strand of plastic just over one inch (2.5 cm) long and slide one socket piece on to it, positioning it in the middle, forming the pelvis. Set the other two sockets aside for now.

5. Bead up some plastic on top of the pelvis socket and Doodle a V shape coming up from the socket at a 45° angle. Each line of the V shape should be about 1.5 inches (3.8 cm) long and about one inch (2.5 cm) apart at the top, as illustrated. Layer up the V shape to reinforce it, so that it's sturdy.

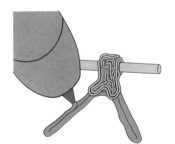

6. To make the armature for the body, string three horizontal lines across the V shape, like a ladder, as illustrated. Note that the pelvis is at the bottom center of the V shape (where it meets in the middle) and the shoulders will be at the top two points of the V shape.

7. To finish the body armature, weld a shoulder joint to the top of one point of the V shape, by welding it at the socket. Be sure that the axle of the shoulder joint is parallel to the axle in the pelvis, as illustrated. Repeat on the other side.

   NOTE: If the inside caps on the shoulder joint axles are touching – that is, at the center of the body armature – they will be too close together to spin freely. Carefully cut them a little shorter and re-cap them with more plastic.

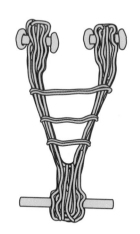

8. Gently lift the body armature away from your Doodling surface and turn it over. Layer up the shoulder sockets so they are more firmly welded to the V shape. Keep the body armature turned over and string a fourth support bar across the widest part of V shape.

9. To complete the hip joints, slide one socket onto the left side of the pelvis and the other onto the right side of the pelvis.

10. Now Doodle a rectangle around the V shape, filling out the body to make it more sturdy. Start at the center bottom where the lines of the V shape meet and Doodle a line that goes out to the side, then up at a perpendicular angle and weld it to the bottom of the shoulder socket, as illustrated. Be sure not to weld the axles to any other pieces. Repeat on the other side, completing the rectangle shape. Reinforce the rectangle.

11. To make a neck joint, repeat steps 1 and 2 to make a single joint, then follow step 3 in order to cap just one end of the axle.

12. The socket of the neck joint should be positioned with the longest side of the rectangle facing the front, so that the short sides can be welded to the top of the shoulder joints. Be sure to weld at the sockets and not over the axle. Now, all joints should be attached, completing the body armature.

Making the limbs and building up the armature

1. To make the armature for the limbs, bead up some plastic on the outside cap of one of the shoulder joints and Doodle a line two inches (5 cm) down, placing a slight bend in it where the elbow would be, as illustrated. Repeat on the other side.

   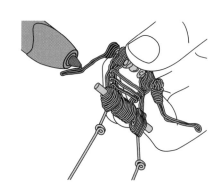

   Now, bead up a little plastic on one of the leg sockets and Doodle a 2.5 inch (6.3 cm) leg, coming down, as illustrated. Be sure to place a slight bend in the middle of it, where the knee would be. Repeat on the other side.

   Reinforce the arms and legs by Doodling over them a few times and layer up the outside of the shoulders, as well. As you layer up the armatures of the arms and legs to strengthen them, you can extend them if you think they are too short, but be sure not to make the limbs too long – or your figure will not be able to stand! String plastic back and forth a few times along the initial arm and leg lines. You will reinforce the armature again later, so just a few new lines is enough.

2. To ensure that the hip sockets stay on the axle, simply press the hot pen tip against the ends of the axle and flatten it, so that ends are wider than the axle. You don't need to extrude any plastic; you can change the shape of the rod using the heat of the 3Doodler's tip. Repeat on the other side.

3. To give the figure feet, Doodle the outline of a foot on your Doodling surface – a rough foot shape is fine but be creative if you want! Be sure to make the footprint wider in the toe and long enough so the figure will be able to stand. Doodle the mirror of the shape to create the second foot. Layer up the outline of both feet a few times to make a sturdy base.

4. Before welding the feet on, make sure the legs are of equal length. Cut one to the correct length, if necessary. Then, hold the figure so that the bottoms of the legs are above the feet and Doodle an ankle by welding each leg to a foot, one at a time. Layer up the feet a few times and be sure that the two parts are firmly connected.

5. Now, strengthen the armature by stringing plastic back and forth across the main body, creating a grid of criss-cross lines – but be very careful not to weld any joints together. Then, layer up the arms and legs by Doodling over all the limbs a few times. You can use any method that reinforces the figure. You can lay the plastic lengthwise, side to side, or you can coil around the limbs. As you do the lower legs, the feet will become more firmly attached as well.

Finally Doodle a cap on top of the axle in the neck joint.

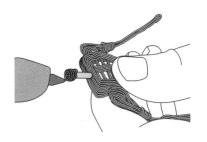

6. Do a final check to make sure all the joints work and there are no weak spots. Layer up weak limbs if necessary. Any loose joints can be tightened by adding a little plastic.

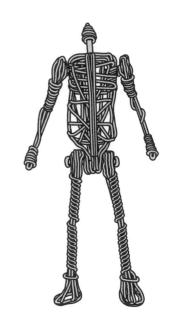

Finishing the figure

1. Now for the most fun part. You can personalize your figure to make any kind of character you want. First, give it a head. To make the head, you can coil on top of the neck joint, or Doodle the basic shape of the head around a balled up piece of tissue, remove the paper and then decorate the exterior.

2. Next, make the hands. You can make each hand as a single shape, like a fist, or you can coil individual fingers. You can also make claws, hammers, hooks, tentacles, weapons or pincers instead of hands!

   NOTE: You can use FLEXY plastic to make the hands, so that they will be able to hold accessories. And, while you have FLEXY in the pen you can give the bottom of the feet better tread and make the figure more stable when standing by pressing FLEXY plastic into the underside of each foot.

3. Finally, Doodle the outer surface of your figure, with any kind of skin, costume or armor! Pick the color you like and decide what the surface texture will be. Will it be fur, muscles, battle armor or a space suit? Be careful not to weld any joints together as you layer up the basic color of the outer skin. Next, you can go back and add details in other colors. You can also use the 3Doodler to weld different materials to the exterior and make yours a mixed media action figure.

You can stop there, or use the 3Doodler and your wild imagination to make accessories. You can craft a backpack, weapons, gear, a helmet, a mask, or a jet pack!

Making your own articulated figure is quite an accomplishment! All the steps in this project are modular, so once you get the hang of it you can do any kind of figure you want – that means different sizes and with as many joints as you choose. Experiment and see if you can find ways to make other kinds of joints. You could even make a character with many more joints for more poses and greater flexibility, then use it for a stop motion movie!

TIP: The armature and joints are much easier to make with ABS because it cools harder, faster and sturdier, but the exterior can be made from ABS, PLA, FLEXY, or even WOOD filament!

TIP: You can weld almost anything on to your figure with the 3Doodler, so, you can use almost any other material to make the outside of the figure. Incorporate bought accessories, or use limbs or parts of other figures and weld them onto yours – as long as they are the same kind of plastic! You can make a robot by welding pieces of metal, paper clips and nuts and bolts to the exterior of your figure and mixing it with Robo Silver PLA. You can buy materials from a craft store, like fabric to give the figure clothes or a cape, faux fur to make an animal or werewolf, cotton balls to make hair, or googly eyes to make your figure completely crazy!

TIP: You can make parts of this project using a desktop 3D printer. 3D print all the limbs and body from 3D computer files and then use the 3Doodler to make the joints and to decorate the figure.

Louis DeRosa

Have you used the 3Doodler to make practical objects like homeware? From decorative to functional items, it's all possible!

Project #17: Vase

For this project, you're going to make a vase that can really hold flowers – and water!

This project might look complex, but it is actually quite simple – you will make a number of rings and then weld them together. A steady hand and a little concentration are all it takes!

We have used Clearly Clear PLA for a sophisticated look, but you can choose whatever plastic you want. Of course, for a tall vase, you will need more plastic, so be sure to stock up. If you want to make the vase waterproof – that is, able to hold water – you will need a clear silicone waterproof sealant (and rubber gloves), which you can get from a hardware store. You also have the option of using an iron.

The stencil is included and we suggest you photocopy it, or download it from the website and then cover it in masking tape to form your Doodling surface. PLA and other plastics will stick easily to paper.

Find stencils at
the3Doodler.com/create/

About making the vase

The vase is made from 61 pieces Doodled from a stencil and then welded together. There are two kinds of pieces: Rings and connector pieces.

- There are 30 thin rings, in six different sizes, plus one thin disc that is fully shaded to create the bottom of the vase

- The connector pieces are four times the thickness of the rings and help make the vase tall

Are you ready?

1. First, Doodle the bottom of the vase. Use the stencil to Doodle and completely fill in circle 1. Then, working from the center out, Doodle from the outer edge of circle 1 to circle 8, with a side-to-side motion, creating a nice texture.

   Reinforce the bottom of the vase. That is, the space inside circle 1.

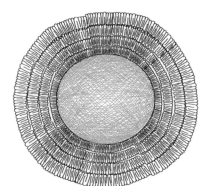

2. Next, make the rings, with a tight side-to-side pen stroke.

   Start with the widest rings first, Doodling from circle 1, out to circle 8 – but don't fill the middle of circle 1 as that is the inside of the vase. Be sure to make the discs flat, even and one layer of plastic only.

   Repeat until you have three in total.

3. Next, make the smallest rings. To do so, repeat the action above, Doodling only from circle 1 to circle 3. Repeat until you have three in total.

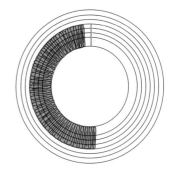

4. Now, make the other four sizes, in quantities of six. To do so, repeat the action above, creating:

    a. Six rings, Doodled from the edge of circle 1 to circle 4

    b. Six rings, Doodled from the edge of circle 1 to circle 5

    c. Six rings, Doodled from the edge of circle 1 to circle 6

    d. Six rings, Doodled from the edge of circle 1 to circle 7

5. Now, you have all 30 rings, plus the bottom of the vase. If any are uneven, place them between two pieces of greaseproof paper and press down on them with an iron on medium heat, like you did for the Birdcage project.

6. To make the connector pieces, use the stencil to Doodle a ring between circle 1 and 2. Repeat until you have four pieces and then weld them together with the pen, so that it is about four times the height of the rings made previously.

   Repeat until you have 30 connector pieces, each made from four rings.

7. Now, it's time to weld the vase together. To so do, weld one ring to one connector, building up as you go in alternate layers, as illustrated. Be sure that there is a connector between each ring.

   To correctly follow the patterns of widest to most narrow ring and then back to wide, stack up all the pieces to match the illustration before welding. Then, start welding from the the base, working up. After you have attached the first few pieces together, reinforce the bottom of the vase and your joins.

   NOTE: Be sure that the hole on the inside of the vase is straight, and that from the outside the pieces look evenly positioned on all sides. When you are halfway through stacking the pieces, it's a good idea to waterproof the lower half of the vase. To do so, put on some protective gloves and then coat the inside of the vase with a translucent silicone waterproof sealant. Do not use the vase until the sealant has set. Be sure to follow the instructions on the sealant that you use.

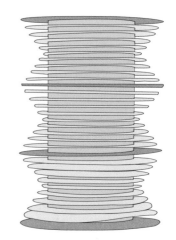

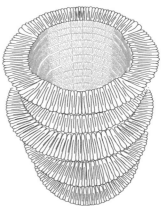

8. Once you have welded all the discs, your vase is almost complete! Trim off any stray bits of plastic and fill any gaps. Use the sealant to waterproof the upper half of the vase

Amazing! Now, you'd better find some flowers to put in the vase!

S

TIP: The vase is modular, so if you want a shorter vase, you don't need to make as many rings and connectors. Look at the illustration in step 7 and decide how tall you want it to be. Check which rings you are removing and don't make them! Then, count how many connectors – or spaces between the rings – you are removing and don't make those either!

TIP: If you have leaks that you can't locate, reseal the vase, following the note in step 7.

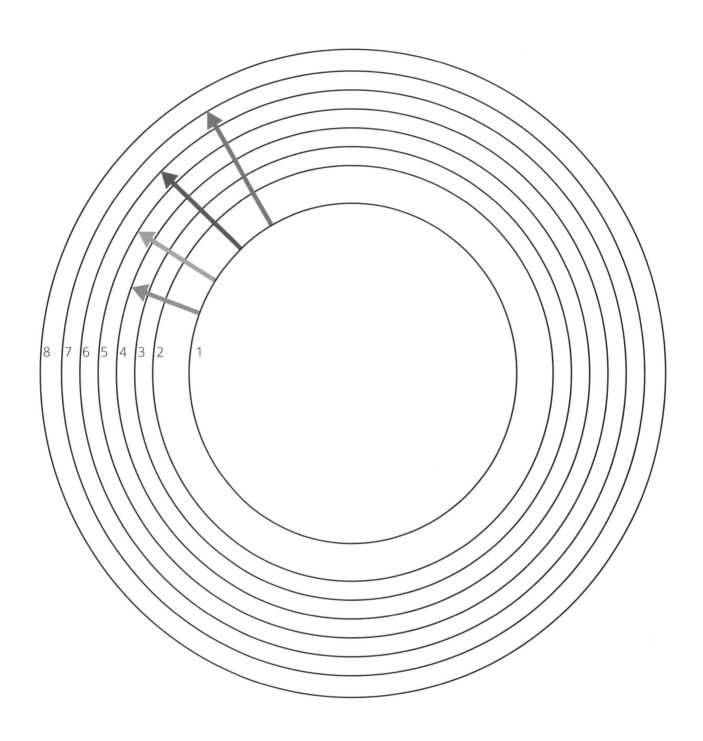

8 7 6 5 4 3 2   1

You've been on quite a journey with your pen and have acquired a considerable amount of skill when it comes to difficult Doodles.

Project #18: Bringing Photos to Life

Now it's time to batten down the hatches and use what you've learned to push your Doodling skills to the limits! A lot of expert Doodlers find inspiration in real life and Doodle what they see. The more difficult Doodling challenges will make you a better Doodler (practice makes perfect!). You will form your own Doodling techniques along the way, from making your own stencils to thinking outside the box about how to achieve the right shape, finish, support, strength – or whatever your Doodle needs to make it picture perfect. As you become part of the 3Doodler Community, you will notice that while everyone has their own handwriting, every Doodler has their own Doodlewriting.

Pirate Ship

One of the most exciting projects we experienced at the 3Doodler office was the making of a ship, based on a photo found in a book. Often, there's no right or wrong way to Doodle something and no right or wrong place to start.

In this project, the main body of the ship was built first, starting with the upper deck, sides and golden captain's quarters as flat Doodles, before being welded together, working from the back to the front.

You will have seen unused strands of plastic used throughout this book before, as axles – never hesitate to use what's around you to help support your Doodle – it really works!

The masts were created from seven strands of unused plastic and welded using a tip from the Windmill project – using the heat of the nozzle to help you push an unused plastic strand through a Doodled part and then reinforcing it with more plastic underneath.

Once that was done, the hull was built (on a real boat, the hull is made first) – and that took a lot of strategic thought, to make sure the ship would be really strong.

The sails were added last, using FLEXY to create the sails by Doodling on flat paper and then attaching unused strands at both the top and bottom of the sail. A bit of slack was left in the sail when it was attached to the mast so that they would curve like real fabric sails do.

The decorative parts, like the railings and ladders, were added at the end as they are more delicate, and creating the main structure comes first.

There are all kinds of extravagant Doodles you can create. Remember, like any art piece, there's a lot of trial and error and you can always cut pieces off and re-Doodle to your heart's content.

Ahoy me hearties, here are some tips!

TIP: When creating free hand Doodles without a stencil, try creating a grid first to get the exact shape right. You can also adjust Doodles with your fingers. Once you're happy with the shape, fill in your Doodle.

TIP: Don't be afraid to use the tools around you to build out your Doodles. In our example of a ship, strands form masts and axles, but pen lids could form cannons, or you could even take accessories from action toys!

TIP: Use a variety of colors to contrast the different elements of your Doodle. Or, add trimmings just to make all the individual colors pop out a little more.

TIP: Sometimes it's better to Doodle parts and then weld them together to get the accurate shape and size you need. For instance, the ship's decks and sides were made in stages. Ladders, hatch doors, anchors and sails were also Doodled on a flat Doodling surface.

Faraz Warsi

HOLIDAYS

Everybody loves holidays and festivities! One of the most fun ways to get ready is to adorn your house with home-made decorations – something the 3Doodler is perfect for, whether you're starting from scratch or personalizing something you bought.

Some of these projects include stencils. We suggest you photocopy the stencil, or download it from the website and then cover it in masking tape to form your Doodling surface. PLA and other plastics will stick easily to paper.

Find stencils at
the3Doodler.com/create/

Project #19: Day of the Dead Sugar Skull

Known for its decorative costumes, altars and statues honoring the dead and celebrating the endless cycle of life, one of the most popular Day of the Dead icons is the sugar skull, or calavera. Traditionally made from sugarcane, these tiny skulls are adorned with traditional motifs, which include paisleys, flowers, teardrops, dots, hearts, flames, fleur-de-lis and many others. You can look online for more inspiration!

You can't Doodle on sugar because it would melt, but you can 3D print your own skull and create amazing festive designs with your 3Doodler!

For this project, you will need access to a regular desktop 3D printer – or if you don't have one you can buy a plastic or ceramic skull. You will also need some paper and colored pencils, or markers, and several colors of plastic: We've used black, red, blue and green.

Erin Song

1. Look online for a 3D file of a skull and print it (or buy one ready-made).

2. Plan your design on paper first, considering what colors you will use and where. Follow our example or go rogue and make your own patterns!

3. If you used ABS for the 3D printed skull, use an ABS strand in your pen (for a PLA skull, use PLA). Anchor the plastic firmly to the skull and Doodle the outline of your design on the skull in black.

4. Fill in the outlined areas with the colors, one color at a time.

Your celebratory 'sugar' skull is one of a kind – and it won't attract sugar-loving pests! You can stop there, or make a few more and experiment with different colors, designs and even other materials – like glitter or metal!

TIP: You don't have to limit yourself to decorations that are flat against the surface of the skull. You can also Doodle up into the air and have many three dimensional elements that leap off the skull.

TIP: Even outside of festivals, the 3Doodler is an amazing and powerful tool for augmenting or fixing 3D prints! You can seamlessly personalize or alter anything you print, or anytime something goes wrong with a print, you can fix it with the 3Doodler.

Project #20: Autumn Leaves

Autumn leaves look good any time – not just during the holidays! Here, we've provided an autumn leaf stencil that will get you in the mood for the coming season!

1. Using one or two colors, Doodle the outline of the leaf, the stem and the veins inside the leaf.

2. Using a new color, fill in the rest of the area inside the leaf.

Kiwib Wong

TIP: You can try the traditional colors of red, yellow, orange, gold and brown – or use crazy colors like purple, blue, green or even glow in the dark – to make impossible leaves that only the 3Doodler could create!

S

Jack O'Lantern and FLEXY Zombies: Louis De Rosa; Witch: Kade Chan; Skeleton Pirate: Kade Chan; Skeleton
Centaur: Kade Chan; Ghost: Erin Song; Black Cat: Kitty Wong; Mummy: Kitty Wong; Bat: Jamie Kao

Project #21: Jack O'Lantern

Halloween is another holiday that people love to decorate their homes for. No pumpkins will be harmed during the making of this project – because you're going to Doodle a Jack O'Lantern!

In this project, you will Doodle in the air, upside down, letting gravity shape the plastic. It's a useful trick you can experiment with.

A pair of scissors or wire cutters might be useful and you will need some scrap paper, a pencil or pen and three colors of plastic: We've used Clearly Clementine, Rainforest Green and Tuxedo Black – but use any colors you like.

1. First, make the core of the pumpkin. To do so, Doodle a rectangle that is four inches (10 cm) long and 0.25 inches (0.5 cm) wide, extending the short sides forming a shape like an apple core for your armature, as illustrated. Fill it in and layer it up so that it's sturdy.

2. To create a frame for the pumpkin, you will need to Doodle in the air. Gently lift the core off your Doodling surface and hold it up with one hand. Using the other hand, bead up some plastic at one end of the core and Doodle a semicircle which connects with the other end of the core, as illustrated.

    NOTE: The semicircle doesn't have to be perfect because pumpkins aren't perfect, so let the plastic hang and harden naturally.

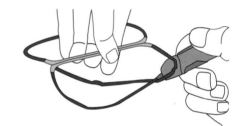

3. Rotate the core in your hand and repeat step 2, placing each new semicircle next to the last one and following a similar shape. Doodle at least six semicircles around the core, creating an armature for your pumpkin.

4. Once you have at least six semicircles, check if they have hardened too far apart, adding in semicircles where there are large gaps. For a strong pumpkin, make at least ten semicircles.

    NOTE: To make a realistic pumpkin, the lines should be slightly different shapes. If you are unhappy with some of your lines, you can cut them off and redo them.

5. To make the skin of the pumpkin, fill the gaps between the semicircles, one by one, stringing plastic side to side. Start at the top and work down, keeping the lines as even as you can.

    NOTE: Be sure to Doodle a strong anchor point without melting the semicircles.

    Repeat until every segment of the pumpkin is filled in.

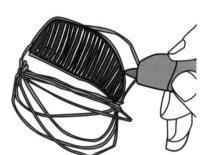

6. Place the pumpkin upright on a flat surface, using the flattest side as the bottom. Layer up the pumpkin more, filling in any gaps in the skin, making the bottom a little flatter and the top a little pointier.

7. Use green plastic (we've used Rainforest Green PLA) to coil a curved stem on the top of the pumpkin, as illustrated. Add a few curly vines coming out from the base of the stem.

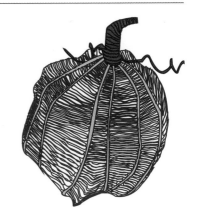

8. It's time to add a face that will turn the pumpkin into a Jack O'Lantern. We've chosen the classic triangle-shaped eyes and nose, but you can create any kind of face you like. It might be best to sketch out your idea on a piece of paper before you Doodle it.

    Use black plastic (we've used Tuxedo Black PLA) to Doodle the outline of the eyes, nose and mouth on the surface of the pumpkin. Next, carefully fill in the eyes, nose and mouth. The mouth is the most difficult, so refer to your sketch or improvise as you Doodle on the uneven surface of the pumpkin.

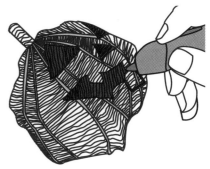

Spooooooooky – well done! Now it's time to put the Jack O'Lantern somewhere it can delight (or scare) trick-or-treaters! Why not Doodle an array of Jack O'Lanterns in different sizes with all kinds of fun or scary faces? You could use any color you like!

TIP: To make the Jack O'Lantern glow, cut a small hole near the bottom in the back, and insert a tiny LED light. Just don't use a real candle!

TIP: 3Doodler's Glow in the Dark PLA is perfect for making scary ghosts, cobwebs and other halloween items.

Louis DeRosa

Project #22: Thanksgiving Turkey

For this project, you're going to make a turkey. Some of the turkey will be made free hand and you'll need a balled up piece of tissue paper as well as the stencil provided. We suggest you photocopy it, or download it from our website and use it to form your Doodling surface.

1. To make the tail, use dark brown plastic and trace over the stencil, starting with the outline. Then fill it in, starting at the bottom in the middle, Doodling a straight line to the edge, then back to the center. Go line by line until you have a neatly filled in tail.

2. To create the white trim at the top of the tail, Doodle short up and down strokes following the arced shape of the tail. Then, create the tail decorations by using light brown plastic to repeat the same action just below the white trim and again about half way down the tail, always following the arc shape.

3. Gently lift the tail off the Doodling surface and decorate the back with white lines from the center to the edge and light brown feather lines at the edge, as illustrated.

4. To make the turkey's body, load the 3Doodler with dark brown plastic. Ball up a piece of tissue paper so that it is about 2.75 inches (7 cm) long and just over two inches (5.5 cm) wide and wind lines of plastic around it until you have a rough armature to build upon.

   Be sure to take the balled up paper out, before the armature becomes too dense.

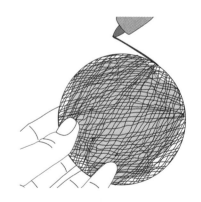

5. After you have removed the balled up piece of tissue paper, keep winding plastic until you have an opaque shell. You can make one side a little wider to form the back and the other side more narrow to form the front – so the overall shape is egg-like.

   Flatten out the back a little, so that you have a flatter surface when you later attach the tail.

   To finish the body, Doodle a few feathers sticking off the top of the body, at the back, as illustrated.

6. Weld the tail to the back of the turkey's body, securely.

7. To make the turkey's neck, roll a small piece of paper to the size of a typical chapstick and wind light brown plastic around it, about one inch (2.5 cm) long. As it starts to become solid, remove the paper and keep winding until you have a solid cylinder.

8. At the end of the neck, free hand the head with a pointy end for the beak, as illustrated. Then, weld the neck to the front of the turkey's body.

9. Follow the stencil provided to Doodle two feet and on each, coil up, Doodling a short and sturdy leg. Attach the legs to the turkey one by one, testing the best position for the second one to create a balanced turkey. For instance, one leg might be further forward than the other.

10. To make the wings, use the stencil provided, filling it in with the same light brown plastic that you used to decorate the tail. Then, weld the wings to either side of the turkey's body.

11. Now, it's time to finish the turkey's face. Load the pen with red plastic and Doodle the wattle coming down from the sides of the beak. Finally, load the pen with black or dark brown and Doodle the eyes by making small dots.

Congratulations, your turkey is finished! But, there's still one thing left to do: Set the table and place your amazing 3Doodled turkey in the middle! Now, where's that cranberry sauce?

S

TIP: You can give the turkey different poses by changing the angle of his legs and toes, but make sure he can balance when he stands. It's normal for this step to be tricky so it's okay to cut off and re-attach the legs a few times.

Front

Back

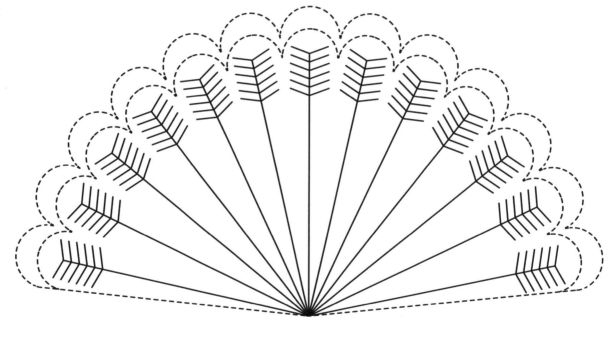

Thanksgiving Turkey: Erin Song; Leaves: Kiwib Wong

Christmas

Christmas is a magical time of year when we love to decorate our homes with distinctive characters and artwork. Sounds like a good excuse to get the 3Doodler out.

The thought that goes into making ornaments and gifts with the 3Doodler is always appreciated! And when it comes to decorating your tree, what could be better than hand crafted ornaments?

You are going to make some Christmas tree ornaments. You will need several colors of translucent PLA as well as brown, white, flesh tone, red, black and orange plastic, some balled up tissue paper, a pen or marker and a pair of scissors.

Project #23: Bauble

1. Using a balled up piece of tissue paper about two to four inches (5-10 cm) in diameter, wind translucent PLA around the paper, until you have an armature for a sphere.

2. Carefully slip the paper out of the framework and finish Doodling around it until you have filled in the surface of the bauble. Try filling it in completely, or give it a grid-like covering, or some other decorations!

    NOTE: If the paper doesn't slip out easily, cut a small hole in the armature, remove the paper and weld it back together.

3. Doodle a loop on the top by bending a line of plastic around a pen or similar object, so you can hang your bauble from your tree.

Nice work! You can make as many baubles as you like, why not experiment with different fun colors?

TIP: You can use more than one color to make a single bauble. With translucent PLA, this will create a lovely effect when light passes through the ornament!

Erin Song

Project #24: Reindeer

Santa needs help delivering all those gifts! Why not Doodle some reindeer friends? You can design the reindeer to be a tabletop decoration, or a hanging ornament. We've used brown plastic but choose any color you wish.

For this project you'll only need your 3Doodler, plastic and a Doodling surface, but scissors may be helpful. Note that this is similar to Doodle dog in the Bootcamp section of the book.

1. Doodle a wide foot on your Doodling surface and then coil a leg coming up from the foot.

2. Repeat this step three times to create four legs of equal height. You might want to sketch where you will Doodle the feet on your Doodling surface first. Determine the size of the reindeer by how far apart you space the feet and how high you make the legs.

3. Once you have all four legs, Doodle a frame for the body by forming a rectangle between the tops of the legs, as illustrated. String an X shape through the rectangle for stability.

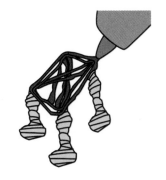

4. Fill out the reindeer's body by layering it up or coiling around the frame between the legs.

5. Coil a little neck, head and snout at the front of the reindeer's body, then layer up the whole reindeer to make it a bit smoother. Doodle a short tail on the back as well.

6. To make the antlers, simply Doodle any shape antlers you want on your Doodling surface and then weld them to the head with the pen.

   NOTE: You can free hand the antlers, or draw your own stencil first.

7. Finally, give the Reindeer a nose. Use red if he needs to shine a light for Santa's sleigh, or another color depending on which of Santa's reindeer you want him to be.

Great stuff, you'll be ready to get your sleigh off the ground in no time!

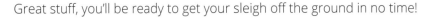
TIP: To make your reindeer appear to be flying, hang them from your tree using Clearly Clear PLA to form a loop.

Project #25: Santa Ornament

Let's build on the bauble method to make a Santa ornament. You will need a balled up piece of tissue paper and a marker pen or similarly shaped item.

1. To make Santa's head, use a flesh tone plastic and repeat the steps from the Bauble project using balled up tissue paper to make a sphere to Doodle around.

2. Use white to Doodle Santa's beard, eyes, eyebrows and the bottom of his hat, as illustrated, leaving room between the moustache and beard for his mouth. Note that his beard should only cover the front half of the ball (his face), but the white band of his hat should go all the way around the Doodle.

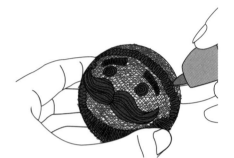

3. Use red to fill in the rest of the hat. Use a pen or similar object to bend a line of plastic around, creating a loop that comes about one inch (2.5 cm) up above the top of his head, forming the shape of his hat, as illustrated.

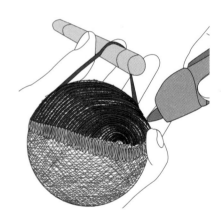

4. String more support lines from the base of the hat to the top and then fill them in completely to make a solid hat.

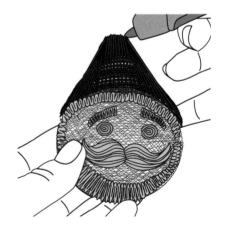

5. Give Santa rosey cheeks and a smiling mouth, in red.

6. Use white to Doodle a white loop coming up from the top of his hat, forming a loop with which to hang him on the tree.

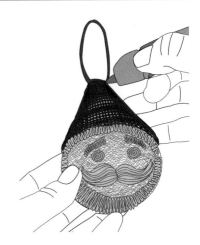

7. Finally, use some black plastic to give his eyes pupils.

Ho, ho, ho! Your Christmas just got a lot more jolly!

> TIP: If you don't want to use the traditional colors we've used, you can get creative and make a bunch of Santas in an array of wild colors. If you want to make some friends for Santa, you can use the same methods to make any kind of face, including elves or reindeer!

Congratulations! You have completed an amazing assortment of holiday decorations!

There are many more ornaments you can make. Why not choose a few other classic Christmas ornaments and figure out how to make them with the 3Doodler? You could decorate your whole tree with items you've made yourself!

Erin Song

Erin Song

> TIP: If you want any of these ornaments to glow, cut a small hole in them and place a small light inside, or attach them to a string of Christmas lights. Be sure to use LED bulbs, as they tend to be cooler and won't melt the plastic.

Menorah: Kitty Wong; Dreidel decoration: Maxwell Bogue

The 3Doodler is a great way to personalize 3D prints – the kind made with a desktop 3D printer – just Doodle onto your 3D print.

Project #26: Hanukkah Dreidel

For Hanukkah, we thought it would be fun to 3D print your own dreidel and decorate it. Dreidel is a traditional game of chance, played during Hanukkah, in which players spin a four sided top and win a prize depending on which side lands facing up.

For this project, all you will need is access to a desktop 3D printer, your 3Doodler and some holiday spirit.

NOTE: Don't have a desktop 3D printer? This project will work just as well with a store bought plastic dreidel, as long as you use the same type of plastic in your 3Doodler.

1. Look online for a 3D file of a dreidel and print it. Your print should be plain and in only one color.

2. Using the same kind of plastic as you used for the 3D printed dreidel – for example, an ABS strand for an ABS print – choose a color to decorate the dreidel with – a metallic filament will look very festive!

3. Decorate your 3D printed dreidel by filling in the Hebrew letters, one by one.

4. Add more elaborate designs, if you want to.

Mazel tov! You can now celebrate an ancient holiday with a toy created using cutting edge technology. Spin the dreidel and see what you win!

TIP: When you fill in the letters on the dreidel, you can layer them up so they feel like embossed letters.

Through their Doodling journey, some 3Doodler artists become so skillful that they make stunning, photorealistic Doodles that are uncannily lifelike. These breathtaking pieces can be made as a purely 3Doodled sculpture, or as the multimedia addition to a flat image.

Niki Fermin uses her 3Doodler to augment her drawings of animals – lifting them off the canvas! It really brings her work to life: Each line of plastic is like the stroke of a pencil, but they build upward – creating an effect that breaks away from traditional drawing.

Moodle (featured below) started life as a regular coloured pencil drawing of a cow. Feeling it was lacking in depth, Niki decided to try Doodling over the nose to give it a sculptural low-relief texture. Using black and white PLA, adding a bit of paint to blend the colors together, the piece gradually came off the paper – and came to life. As a final touch, Niki added some wood at the top and bottom of the canvas to really make Moodle look like a cow sticking its head through a fence. Overlapping the nose with the wood gave it that final lifelike lift.

What could you create if you combined a traditional drawing style with the modern capabilities and 3D texture of the 3Doodler?

Lifelike Doodling: Niki Fermin

ABSTRACT 3DOODLING

Creating abstract work with the 3Doodler is a new experience for artists that simply wasn't possible before the 3Doodler was invented!

Brooklyn based gallery artist, Rachel Goldsmith, is known for the rich forms she weaves together in the incredible "organic abstract" pieces she creates with the 3Doodler. Rachel uses her 3Doodler to literally "paint with plastic", layering intricate lines of different colors, and creating a whole new palette that appears to blend the plastics the way you would blend paint! Her pieces contain a rich topography of vibrant peaks and deep shadows that could never be achieved with brush and paint.

The projects you have seen and done throughout this book range from resembling real to more artistic creations. To really expand your creative horizons and artistic spirit, why not explore abstract work as well?

Abstract Doodling: Rachel Goldsmith

Abstract Doodling: Rachel Goldsmith

GALLERY

For more stunning images, videos and projects from around the world please visit the 3Doodler Community Site at: www.the3Doodler.com/community

#WhatWillYouCreate?™

Birdcage Grid: Marie Rouillon; Figure and Giraffe: Esra Oguz

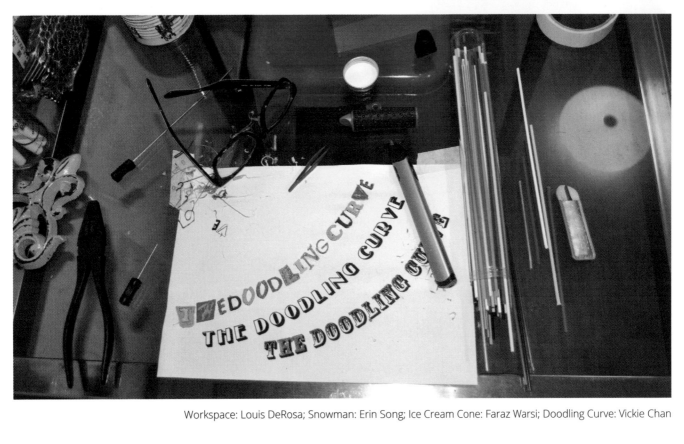

Workspace: Louis DeRosa; Snowman: Erin Song; Ice Cream Cone: Faraz Warsi; Doodling Curve: Vickie Chan

Turkey: Erin Song; Rooster: Marie Rouillon; Fish: Alex Konahin

Dinosaurs: Louis DeRosa; Lion: Esra Oguz

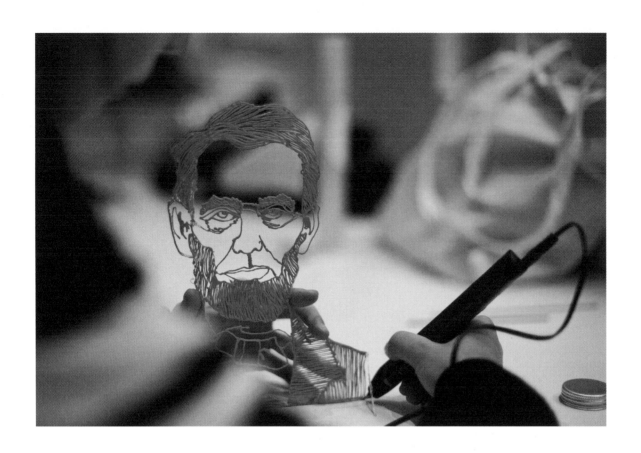

Abraham Lincoln Portrait: Erin Song; Dinosaur Armature: Louis DeRosa

Grace Du Prez

Tong Chan

Panda: Esra Oguz; Bracelet: Grace Du Prez

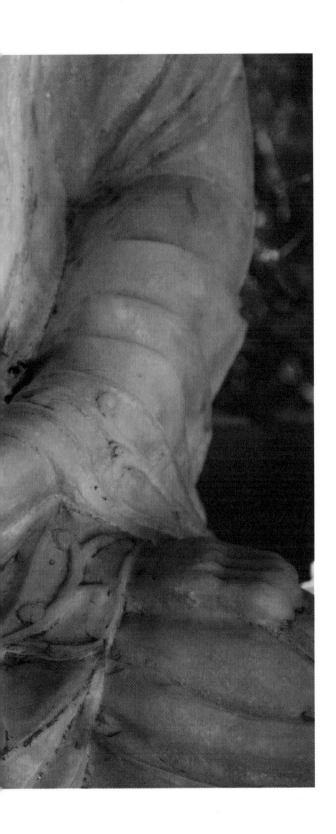

Lotus Flower: Louis DeRosa; Sugar Skull: Erin Song; Day of the Dead Mariachis: Edith Shek

Faraz Warsi

139

Pete Dilworth

Esra Oguz

Marisa Lewis

Jina Sim

Esra Oguz

Marie Rouillon

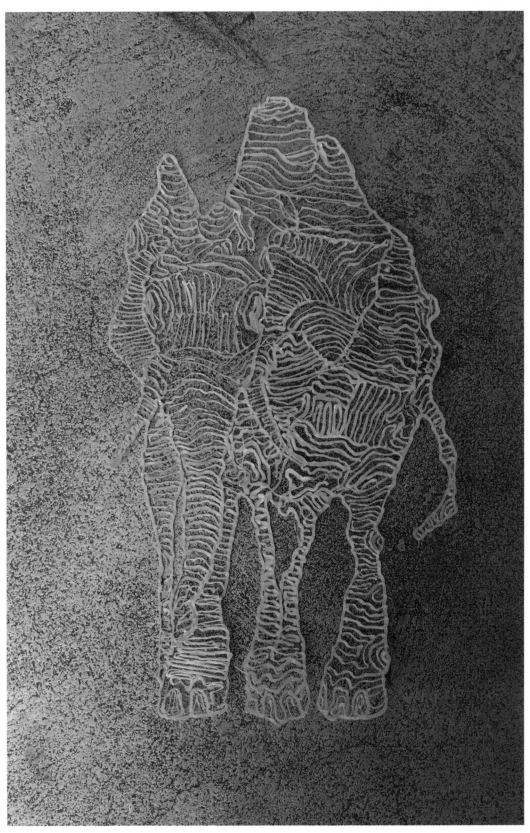

Omar Shammah

Jina Sim

Cornelia Kuglmeier

Stanley Chung

Sara Berti (Project #3)

Sara Berti is an Italian artist known for her solid art techniques and theories, rooted in Italian traditions. Sara's work seeks to open up creative encounters with new cultures. She has received worldwide recognition and represented Italy at the 54th Venice Biennale.

Kade Chan (Gallery)

Kade Chan is a professional origami artist from Hong Kong. Born in 1993, he started folding paper in 2005. Kade has more than 100 original published origami designs and is the recipient of multiple awards, including from the Japan Origami Academic Society.

Tong Chan (Gallery)

Tong Chan is a graphic designer and visual artist from Hong Kong. She has a diverse professional background in design, advertising, editorial graphics and motion works. Pursuing her belief in art as therapy, Tong also works as a drawing tutor for disabled children.

Louis DeRosa (Project #6; #9; #11; #16; #21; Gallery)

Louis DeRosa comes from a family of artists in Buffalo, NY. His love of drawing, coupled with experience in 3D modeling and a degree in animation made the 3Doodler a natural fit for his creative style. Louis's favorite 3Doodler uses are custom action figures and anatomical models.

Niki Fermin (Likelike 3Doodling)

Niki Fermin is a UK-based artist who has more recently focused on drawing animals and pet portraits. Niki was an early user of the 3Doodler and has since merged her artistic passions, creating works such as the Moodle, as well as several 3Doodler commissions.

Nikka Francisco (Project #1; #15; Gallery)

Born and raised in Hong Kong, Nikka Francisco is a visual artist who specializes in graphic design and cartoon drawing. Nikka's work focuses on the exploration of different techniques and mediums, with the aim of creating truly unique designs.

Rachel Goldsmith (Project #3; Abstract 3Doodling)

Rachel Goldsmith is a New York-based artist who works primarily with PLA plastic, water-based paints on canvas or permanent inks on paper. Rachel received her Masters of Art and Design Education from the Pratt Institute in 2007 and has exhibited widely.

Joe James (Project #14)

Based in London, England, Joe is a prop and model maker for the commercial and film industry and also dabbles in illustration. Both jobs enable him to work with different materials every day to discover exciting new processes and techniques.

Cornelia Kuglmeier (Nozzles; Gallery)

Cornelia Kuglmeier was born and lives in Germany. She studied fine arts and art education in Nuremberg. She began Doodling in 2014 and concentrates on three-dimensional figures of humans in motion, fantasy creatures, and creating films with 3Doodled figures.

Bo Lau (Project #5)

Bo Lau is an animation student from Hong Kong. She loves watching cartoons and building cartoon sculptures, passions that are evident in her work and creations using the 3Doodler. Bo's ambition is to work in the creative fields of animation and film production.

Marisa Lewis (Project #10; Gallery)

Marisa Lewis is a UK-based artist, graduating from the University of Worcester with a BA in Illustration as well as Masters in Creative Digital Media. Marisa loves to both create and look at art. Marisa works as a writer and editor for a leading CG art website.

Esra Oguz (Project #3; Gallery)

Esra Oguz is a qualified handcrafts teacher from Turkey, currently working on art renovation and restoration projects in Istanbul. Esra also specializes in ready-to-wear fashion and jewelry and focuses on Doodling with various materials, using innovative techniques.

Grace Du Prez (Project #17; Gallery)

Grace Du Prez is a London-based Designer-Maker who creates one-off statement pieces for both fashion and interiors. Her work develops from a surface and textile-led method, with an experimental approach that uses a variety of tactile materials and processes.

Marie Rouillon (Project #4; #8; Gallery)

Marie Rouillon is a material designer and visual artist from Paris, France. Fascinated by materials and technology, she graduated in 2011 with a Masters in Design for Textile Futures from Central Saint Martins College (London). She lives and works in London, UK.

Edith Shek (Project #19)

Edith is a graphic designer and crafts lover. Her work focuses on how color, form and shape can be used as key stimuli for visual expression. She graduated in 2015 from the visual communication design in Hong Kong Polytechnic University.

Erin Song (Project #7; #19; #22; #23; #24; #25; Gallery)

Erin Song is a Korean artist pursuing a BFA in Graphic Design at Savannah College of Art and Design (SCAD). Erin loves creating intricate line drawings, Doodling (of course), and taking photos of whatever else catches her eye.

Faraz Warsi (Project #12; #18; Gallery)

Faraz Warsi is the Lead Designer at 3Doodler and has been responsible for crafting the 3Doodler design presence since launch. Faraz's work spans web, print and product design, and his 3Doodled creations have been featured in the MoMA Design Store in New York.

Kiwib Wong (Project #2; #20)

Kiwib Wong is a fashion designer from Hong Kong and one of the founders of the SHIGO fashion brand. Kiwib loves to apply unconventional materials and technology in fashion garments. Kiwib is one of the creators of the now famous 3Doodled Seashell Dress.

Kitty Wong (Project #26)

Kitty Wong is an artist and fashion design student. Kitty's focus is experimentation with different materials and craftsmanship in her works. Kitty has been a finalist in numerous fashion shows, including the Hong Kong Young Fashion Designers' Contest (YDC) 2015.

We would also like to thank Maxwell Bogue, Matthew Butchard, Vickie Chan, Stanley Chung, Peter Dilworth, , Jamie Kao, Alex Konahin, Blessy Man, Jina Sim, Omar Shammah, LiHui Ting and SHIGO for their Doodled contributions to this book.

3Doodler®, DoodleStand®, JetPack, StrandStand and "#WhatWillYouCreate?" are trademarks owned by WobbleWorks, Inc.

ISBN 978-0-692-46693-3

Design & layout by Vickie Chan
Edited by Vickie Chan
Written by Joshua Klausner

Cover photograph by Peter Desiderio
Cover Doodle by Blessy Man
Photography by Joshua Klausner
Additional Photography by Faraz Warsi and Vickie Chan

Printed and bound by Everbest Printing Co. Ltd, China

WobbleWorks, Inc.
Suite 153
342 East 14th Street
New York, NY 10009-153
USA
www.the3Doodler.com

Stay up to date with the latest from 3Doodler, including special offers and new projects, at www.the3Doodler.com.

Nikka Francisco and LiHui Ting